A TIME FOR PEACE

A TIME FOR PEACE

MIKHAIL S. GORBACHEV

RICHARDSON & STEIRMAN
NEW YORK
1985

I.S.B.N. 0-931922-08-0

Library of Congress Catalog Number: 85-073296

Design by Larry Alexander
Typography by Dawn Typographic Services, New York

TABLE OF CONTENTS

A TIME FOR PEACE

INTRODUCTION

INTRODUCTION

THIS book is a collection of statements made between March and October 1985, since my election as General Secretary of the Communist Party Central Committee. Its content represents my own and my colleagues' ideas, arising from reflections on the past and the present, a contemplation of the future, and from talks with very different people: factory managers and workers, farmers and scientists, politicians from other countries, my friends, and my critics.

This book naturally reflects this particular historical moment, which not only prompts but, at times, dictates a definite approach to problems facing the Soviet Union, as well as ways of seeking their solution. But the present is so packed with events and changes that sometimes even a single day may be equivalent to a whole epoch in terms of the scope of decisions that have to be made and of the significance of what must be accomplished for present and future generations. This is convincingly demonstrated by the experience of any country.

To a considerable extent, this complex decision-making process is also true of the domestic tasks facing our state which command the attention of the Soviet Union's leadership. We have major achievements as well as quite a few unresolved problems, some of which are very serious. I shall not list them here, as they are dealt with in sufficient detail in this book. I wish to stress only that a country which has set itself the primary task of raising its people's standard of living and quality of life cannot but have a vital stake in peace, in tranquil and normal international affairs, and in mutually advantageous cooperation. Our foreign policy is an organic and logical extension of our domestic policy.

The present-day world situation causes grave anxiety among our people. I believe that these apprehensions are shared by many Americans. Mankind now faces the most crucial choice in civilization's history, a choice that must be made today, before it is too late. It is a choice between further straining international tensions or relaxing them, between escalating the arms race to cosmic proportions or curtailing it, between confrontation or cooperation. A common danger has always required common efforts. This is how our alliance during the war against fascism arose. Today we face a still greater danger: total nuclear annihilation. Can it really be that we lack the wisdom, patience, perseverance, and courage needed to ward off this formidable threat?

The weight of responsibility that history and life itself have imposed on our two countries—on their political leadership—is especially great today. We are firmly committed to returning Soviet-American relations back onto a normal track, back to the road of mutual understanding and cooperation. We favor a negotiated settlement of all disputed issues. The Soviet Union stands ready to seek and find common ground on matters of disarmament and the improvement of the international situation. But, quite clearly, this goal cannot be achieved without reciprocal efforts on the part of the United States.

Peace, peaceful coexistence, equality, and mutually beneficial cooperation are the basic principles of our foreign policy. The Soviet Union seeks neither foreign territory nor foreign resources. We have enough of everything. Besides, the Soviet people know the horrors of war and its tragic aftermath only too well from their own bitter experience.

The vital need for peace and ways of achieving it is a major theme of this book. In addressing the American reader, let me say that our country has never instigated or initiated an arms race. We have not been the first to start manufacturing any type of weapon. The Soviet Union has pledged not to deploy weapons in space if other nations do not do so. We shall not conduct nuclear tests and explosions if the United States joins the moratorium we have declared. We would like this moratorium to be the first step on the road towards reducing and eventually eliminating nuclear weapons.

I would also like to draw your attention to our latest proposals: to reduce nuclear armaments capable of reaching each other's territory by 50 percent if both sides completely prohibit space-based strike weapons; and also, irrespective of this reduction, to reduce medium-range nuclear weapons substantially in Europe. All this, of course, is subject to the strict observance of the principle of equal security and to verification by all necessary measures agreed upon through negotiation.

In conclusion, let me say that our country will never unleash war. This is the position of the Soviet leadership. This is the opinion of the millions of Soviet people engaged in peaceful, constructive work.

As the author of this collection, I would like to thank Richardson and Steirman, who have kindly undertaken to publish this book. I would consider my aim achieved if the American reader gains a better understanding of our plans and intentions, and if he feels our desire for peace and cooperation.

I sincerely wish my American readers prosperity and a peaceful future!

Mikhail Gorbachev
October 1, 1985

1

BIOGRAPHY OF
MIKHAIL GORBACHEV

AT THE March 12, 1985 Plenary Meeting of the Central Committee of the Communist Party held in Moscow, Mikhail Sergeyevich Gorbachev was elected General Secretary of the Central Committee of the Communist Party of the Soviet Union. He was entrusted with the highest post in the political leadership of a country in which nearly 277 million people of more than 100 nationalities live side by side.

In many respects, Mikhail Gorbachev's life is typical of an entire generation of Soviet Communists who make up the nucleus of the party.

Mikhail Gorbachev was born on March 2, 1931, in the village of Privolnoye in Stavropol Territory, a vast region north of the Caucasus mountains. The area is famous for its grain harvest, for its sheep breeding, its power-engineering specialists, chemists, scholars, and doctors. The people of the Stavropol region are an industrious and tenacious people, who for centuries have grown grain and grazed their flocks under difficult, often harsh conditions, but they later built canals, developed industries, and founded cities and health resorts on the arid steppe.

Mikhail Gorbachev's parents came from peasant stock who earned their living by the sweat of their brows. His grandfather, a hard-working and respected man, was the founder and chairman of a collective farm. His father, Sergei Andreyevich, was an agricultural machine operator who had fought at the front in the Great Patriotic War. He was a modest man, deeply respected for his skills and knowledge of economic matters and his wisdom and even-handedness in party affairs.

Mikhail Gorbachev's mother, Maria Panteleyevna, is industrious and well respected. She is seventy-four years old and still lives in the Stavropol region, from which she refuses to be separated.

Mikhail Gorbachev's natural gifts and inquiring mind, his self-discipline and energy, and his love of the land stood out even in childhood. At fourteen, he had already learned to handle a grain combine during the long hours of the strenuous harvest.

When he was eighteen, he was awarded one of the most esteemed Soviet awards: the Order of the Red Banner of Labor.

After finishing secondary school, where he was awarded a silver medal at graduation, he enrolled in the Department of Law at Moscow State University and he received his law degree in 1955. Twelve years after graduation he attended a second institute of higher education — an agricultural institute — and became a specialist in agricultural economics. His many-sided education and continual striving for knowledge are at the root of his approaches to the solution of life's problems.

Early in his youth, Mikhail Gorbachev, the son of a Communist and an active member of the Young Communist League, showed a deep-seated interest in sociopolitical matters. He was able to captivate people with his brilliance and to interest them. He was not embarrassed to learn from friends, to adopt better ideas, and to support new ones. His originality of thought and his charm attracted people to him. At twenty-one he joined the ranks of the CPSU, and by the time he was thirty he was elected for the first time as a delegate to a party congress — the highest governing body of the CPSU.

After graduating from Moscow University, he returned to Stavropol Territory, where he participated actively in developing the youth movement and was elected to executive posts in the Young Communist League. From March 1962 Mikhail Gorbachev was engaged in party work. Over the years, he was promoted consistently to key party posts: First Secretary of a City Party Committee; Second Secretary of a Territorial Committee, and from April 1970, First Secretary of one of the party's most authoritative organizations: that of Stavropol Territory. In March 1971, at the 24th Congress, Mikhail Gorbachev was elected a member of the CPSU Central Committee.

Gorbachev gained experience in Stavropol Territory. It had a highly developed and diversified economy, and he grew there as a citizen and political leader. He had a profound grasp of the problems of agriculture and industry, science and education, health care, and social welfare. During these years, major programs were initiated in Stavropol Territory for developing mechanical engineering, the chemical industry, the construction of resorts, canal building, and the expansion of irrigation. New developments in farming and animal husbandry were also introduced.

In solving complex tasks of production, Mikhail Gorbachev devoted much of his attention to working people. Aware of their needs and concerns, he organized and stimulated the labor process. He was always in the thick of every operation. He spent time with people in factories, shops, farms, and research laboratories. These were the places where he worked, not in his private office or in lecture halls. It was here that he developed his knowledge of people and a deeper knowledge of life.

His fields of interest are very wide. Mikhail Gorbachev is interested in literature and theater. He studies new works in political economy, philosophy, law, and art with intense concentration. He travels around the Soviet Union and visits foreign countries frequently.

In 1978 a plenary meeting of the Central Committee of the CPSU elected Mikhail Gorbachev Secretary of the Central Committee. Two years later, he was elected a member of the Politburo. For the last fifteen years, voters have entrusted him with the mandate of people's deputy to the highest body of power. Since 1985 he has been a member of the Presidium of the Supreme Soviet of the USSR, a permanent body of state power.

In his work in the highest bodies of party and government, the creative side of Mikhail Gorbachev's character—as a Communist, politician and organizer—has revealed itself most fully. His style and method of his work are reminiscent of the style and method bequeathed to party leaders by Lenin: collective leadership and ability to analyze a situation profoundly, to know people's views, to learn from the past, to pursue a charted course, to unite people, and to live in their interests.

Because of his work, his devotion to duty, his conviction, his ability to convince others, his consistency of action and fighting spirit, his skill in grasping the essence of issues and his rejection of meaningless routine, his democracy and humane sympathy, Mikhail Gorbachev has won the highest award in Soviet society: the confidence and respect of the party and the people.

Soviet society and its economy have always been characterized by dynamism. The rate of industrial growth in the USSR in the postwar years was twice as great as that of developed capitalist countries. Since the beginning of the 1970s, however, the country has experienced difficulties in economic development. Radical changes in the economic situation were not taken adequately into account. The persistence necessary to reorganize structural policies, the forms and methods of administration, and the very psychology of economic activity was not present. The party and the people were confronted with the task of surmounting these negative tendencies in order to sharply change the state of affairs for the better.

At the April 1985 Plenary Meeting of the CPSU Central Committee, Mikhail Gorbachev delivered a report on the new tasks of the party and the people. The provisions of the report, the interest and discussion they provoked, and the decisions of the plenary meeting marked a turning point in the development of our country. Soviet society has entered a period of qualitative changes in its economic and social life.

In implementing the course set by the April plenary meeting, the Central Committee and the Soviet Government have worked out large-scale measures for a wide range of issues that will affect the restructuring of the national economy. The General Secretary of the Central Committee has conducted a series of business meetings with party and economic leaders, directors of enterprises, scientists and specialists. In keeping with good party tradition, he consulted with rank-and-file workers, with those who directly produce material benefits. His meetings with Muscovites and Leningraders, his trips to the Ukraine and Byelorussia, to talk with the oil workers of Siberia and the grain growers of the virgin lands in Kazakhstan had an enormous social impact, aiding the active implementation of the course worked out by the party.

The Central Committee sees the situation in the following way: The national economy must be brought in the shortest possible time to the most advanced scientific and technological positions, to the highest world level in productivity. We must learn to properly use all the advantages and possibilities that socialism gives us in order to obtain substantially greater results with fewer expenditures. To achieve this goal, we must free ourselves from economic methods that have exhausted their usefulness and succeed in breaking through to qualitative heights in science and technology, and on this basis make our country more powerful and richer materially and culturally. This is the main task facing Soviet society at the moment.

It has been stated justifiably that foreign policy is an extension of domestic policy. In Soviet politics this relationship is organic and indissoluble. The Soviet Union strives for broad and multifaceted cooperation with all the governments of the world, particularly socialist countries. Our principle is equal and beneficial relations, assistance in developing natural resources, and strengthening friendship among peoples.

What changes in the world would the Soviet Union consider beneficial to it? First of all—an end to the arms race—the elimination of the threat of nuclear war. Every ruble it spends on defense it would rather spend on peaceful needs, on improving the well-being of working people. Obviously, the United States and other capitalist countries can also find better uses for the money currently being spent on the manufacture of arms. It is important to take into account the problems faced by developing countries. The Soviet Union's reason for insisting on an end to the arm's race is the fact that it is immoral to throw away hundreds of billions of dollars on the creation of the means to annihilate human beings when hundreds of millions of people are hungry, deprived of life's essentials.

It is precisely from this standpoint that Mikhail Gorbachev announced the suspension of all Soviet atomic explosions on August 6, 1985. The suspension will remain in effect until January 1, 1986, or beyond that date if the USA also refrains from conducting nuclear tests. The USSR has called on the USA to resume negotiations for a total ban on nuclear tests. The Soviet leader believes that the total ban on nuclear tests would stop the arms race at its most dangerous point—the development of qualitatively new weapons—and would be a serious contribution to preserving and strengthening the policy of nonproliferation of nuclear weapons.

Great attention is paid in the USSR to Soviet-American relations. The state of these relations is vitally important for mankind and has an enormous influence on the international situation as a whole.

It is the deep-seated conviction of the General Secretary of the CPSU Central Committee that confrontation is not an inherent defect in the relations between the USSR and the USA. Instead it is an anomaly, a condition that is lacking in all logic. Differences in social systems provide absolutely no reasons for bad relations, let alone for inspiring enemity. In its dealing with all states, the USSR pursues a policy of peaceful coexistence. In this way, each of the social systems can prove which is the better by the strength of its example and not by the strength of its arms. The General Secretary emphasizes that this is the credo of the USSR.

Peace is the most important goal of the Communist Party and the Soviet state. This is demonstrated by Mikhail Gorbachev's announcement, in the name of Soviet leadership and people, that it will never originate war in the Soviet Union and the Soviet state will never start a war.

In his public appearances, Mikhail Gorbachev has repeatedly expressed his concern about burning conflicts in various parts of the world. In his view, sites of tension in Asia, Africa, and Latin America could be eliminated and peace restored if every member of the UN Security Council undertook the responsibility of honoring the principles of noninterference, non-use of force, and noninvolvement of the countries on these continents in military blocs.

The Soviet Union's position on this issue has been formulated precisely and clearly: We are opposed to policies of threats and violence, to violations of human rights—especially such sacred ones as the right to life and work. We are opposed to having liberated and developing countries become a source that enriches monopolies, or be used for establishing military bases as springboards for aggression. We state openly and clearly: The Soviet Union is on the side of those who struggle for peace, national independence, and social justice.

Since the Great October Revolution, the first day of its birth, the land of the Soviets has advocated a world without wars and weapons, a world of social justice. The Communist Party and the Soviet Government have consistently and purposefully subordinated their policy to this ideal, and it is to this ideal that Mikhail Gorbachev has dedicated his life and his energy.

Mikhail Gorbachev's wife, Raisa, is a graduate of the Department of Philosophy of Moscow State University. She is a Candidate of Science in philosophy and is a senior lecturer. Their daughter, Irina, is a physician, a Candidate of Science in medicine. Her husband, Anatoli, is a surgeon. The Gorbachevs' granddaughter, Ksenia, is six years old.

2

FROM THE SPEECH
AT THE EXTRAORDINARY
PLENARY MEETING
OF THE CPSU
CENTRAL COMMITTEE

In the foreign-policy sphere, our course is clear and consistent. It is the course of peace and progress.

A basic principle of our party and state is to preserve and strengthen in every way the fraternal friendship with our closest friends and allies—the countries of the great socialist community. We will do everything in our power to expand cooperation with socialist states, to enhance the role and influence of socialism in world affairs. We would like to see a considerable improvement of relations with the People's Republic of China and believe that, given reciprocity, such improvement is quite possible.

The Soviet Union has always supported the struggle of the peoples for liberation from colonial oppression. Today our sympathy is with the countries of Asia, Africa, and Latin America, which are following the road of consolidating their independence and social rejuvenation. For us they are friends and partners in the struggle for a durable peace, for better and just relations between nations.

As for relations with capitalist states, we will firmly follow the Leninist course of peace and peaceful coexistence. The Soviet Union will always respond to goodwill with goodwill, to trust with trust. But everyone should know that we shall never relinquish the interests of our Motherland and those of our allies.

We value the successes of détente achieved in the 1970s and are ready to take part in carrying on the process of establishing peaceful, mutually beneficial cooperation between nations following the principles of equality, mutual respect, and noninterference in internal affairs. New steps along these lines would be appropriate in marking the fortieth anniversary of the great victory over Hitler's fascism and Japanese militarism.

Never before has so terrible a threat hung over mankind as now. The only reasonable way out of the existing situation is for the opposing forces to reach an agreement on the immediate termination of the arms race—the nuclear arms race on earth and the prevention of an arms race in space. We need an agreement on an honest and equitable basis without attempts at "outplaying" the other side and dictating terms to it. We need an agreement that would help everyone advance toward the cherished goal — the complete elimination and prohibition of nuclear weapons for all time — toward the complete removal of the threat of nuclear war. This is our firm conviction.

Negotiations between the Soviet Union and the United States will open in Geneva tomorrow. The approach of the Soviet Union to these negotiations is well known. I shall reaffirm only this: We do not strive for unilateral advantages, for military superiority over the United States, over NATO countries; we want a termination, not a continuation of the arms race and therefore propose a freeze of nuclear arsenals and an end to further deployment of missiles; we want a real and substantial reduction of the arms stockpiles — not the development of ever-new weapons systems in space or on earth.

We would like our partners in the Geneva negotiations to understand the Soviet Union's position and reciprocate. Then agreement will be possible, and the peoples of the world would heave a sigh of relief.

March 11, 1985

3

LENINISM:
A LIVING AND
CREATIVE SCIENCE

COMRADES! The CPSU Central Committee and the Soviet Government are carrying out a vast amount of work in order to preserve and strengthen peace. Implementing the line of the 26th Party Congress and working for the fulfillment of the Peace Program for the 1980s, we stand for a reasonable organization of international relations, above all those designed to avert war. The latest Soviet peace initiatives, put foward by Comrade Yuri Andropov, reflect a sincere desire to bring back détente and open up new possibilities for the consolidation of the norms of peaceful coexistence in international life.

Each step taken by the Soviet Union, each of our initiatives is an embodiment of Lenin's behests. His peace strategy, his principles of socialist foreign policy determine all the international activities of the CPSU and the Soviet state.

The time we live in will go down in history as a time of intense class struggle in the world arena. There are sharp clashes between two lines, two diametrically opposed approaches to international relations.

The adventurist approach of the most aggressive forces of imperialism to the main question of our time—the question of war and peace—is the chief cause of the present aggravation of the international situation. Lenin said: "... An issue... of war and peace cannot properly be posed if the class antagonisms of modern society are lost sight of...." Imperialist reaction can hide behind many masks, but it cannot hide the fact that its foreign course is dictated, even today, by narrowly selfish class interests.

The striving for maximum profits, for the perpetuation of a society of oppression and exploitation, and for world domination is the real basis of imperialism. Lenin's characterization of imperialism and of the forces that motivate its policy retains all its significance in our time.

The capitalist system is in the throes of a deep crisis which has

---

The excerpt of this speech was included in the book because of its significance.

engulfed the economy and politics and the material and spiritual life of bourgeois society. The contradictions between labor and capital, among the imperialist and the liberated states, and among the power centers within the capitalist world are being exacerbated. The most die-hard circles of imperialist bourgeoisie lay the blame for the overall weakening of the exploiter society not on its internal contradictions, not on the internal logic of its development, but on socialism and its international policy.

In these conditions a reactionary trend has triumphed within the U.S. ruling circles and, in Lenin's words, a "war party" which "says to itself: Force must be used immediately, irrespective of possible consequences" has taken the upper hand. The most aggressive circles of imperialism—and, above all, of U.S. imperialism—are trying to clamber out of the crisis, to find the answer to the historic challenge of socialism by continuing the arms race and by building up the threat of war.

The aggressive aspirations of imperialism are directed primarily against the Soviet Union and the entire socialist community. Economic sanctions, psychological warfare, attempts to organize a "crusade" against communism, interference in the internal affairs of socialist states, including the nurturing of a counterrevolutionary "fifth column," as was done in Poland, for example—all these are real and irrefutable facts.

As in the past, imperialist reaction is eager to rewrite history, to push back world socialism, to slow down the peoples' liberation movements. Essentially, socialism is being presented with an ultimatum: If it does not give up its positions, the whole situation will deteriorate in the direction of war. But the alternative—either to obey the dictate of imperialism on a worldwide scale or to face a world war—is mad and monstrous in its very essence.

Our socialist approach to international problems, which embodies the working people's cardinal interests, is opposed to the policy of imperialism and the imperialist approach. We are convinced that social progress cannot be stopped, that the historic process of mankind's transition to socialism cannot be impeded, and that socialism means peace.

There are no forces in the Soviet Union and the fraternal

socialist countries that need war, the arms race, and the aggravation of the world situation. Peace, détente, universal security, fair and mutually beneficial cooperation, and the inviolability of the right of the nations of the world to social and national progress, to independent determination of their own destiny—such are our clear and openly stated goals. Leonid Brezhnev said in the Central Committee's report to the 26th Congress that the Peace Program elaborated by the CPSU remained, as before, a reliable compass in the struggle for a cardinal improvement of the international situation.

The growing unity of the fraternal socialist states, their close cohesion and loyalty to the principles of Marxism-Leninism and socialist internationalism are a most important factor in the struggle for peace. The Prague meeting of the Political Consultative Committee of the Warsaw Treaty member states demonstrated once again these countries' resolve to bar the road to war.

We regard the curbing of the arms race, which is now entering a qualitatively new, much more dangerous phase, as the central task in the struggle to avert war. Ignoring the interests of the world's peoples, the U.S. administration is behaving irresponsibly and is planning to continue an unrestrained buildup of the stockpiles of nuclear weapons and to carry on an unbridled race in all types of strategic arms. Under the cover of "zero option," "intermediate option," and other pretexts, the U.S. militarists are pressing forward, placing their stake on the deployment of their medium-range missiles in Western Europe, come what may, thereby turning the peoples of the region into nuclear "hostages" of the United States. To this day the United States and its NATO partners have not responded to the unilateral step taken by the Soviet Union not to be the first to use nuclear weapons.

The Soviet Union has countered American attempts to use the talks to destroy the existing balance of forces with a constructive proposal on a mutual reduction of arms whereby, as a first step, the general balance would be maintained, but at the lowest possible levels. In working toward disarmament—especially nuclear disarmament—our country does not seek military supremacy.

We sincerely hope that the talks on the limitation and reduction of strategic arms and on the problem of medium-range nuclear weapons in Europe will be successful. We are prepared to reach agreement on the basis of reciprocity, consideration of the legitimate interests of both sides, and in keeping with the principle of equality and equal security. Is that not an honest approach, and does it not testify to our goodwill?

The might of the defensive alliance of the Warsaw Treaty countries safeguards peace and the gains of socialism. And as long as the situation requires, the peoples of the socialist community will continue, as before, to do everything necessary to make their defense stronger and even more effective. The Soviet armed forces, supported by the love of the entire Soviet people and the concern of the CSU and the Soviet state, are safeguarding vigilantly the peaceful life of the Soviet people, of the entire community of the fraternal socialist countries. Those who are fond of adventures should not forget this. As Lenin put it, "We will be able to stand up for ourselves; we were not beaten, and we will not be beaten or deceived."

Comrades! The U.S. imperial ambitions, the arms race, the cult of force, war propaganda—all that makes the imperialist approach to international problems a universal danger. As we know, the aggressive stand of the ruling circles of the Western camp is opposed by a more realistic, sober stand whose advocates favor détente and cooperation. The development of relations between the Soviet Union and many Western countries shows that we have many fields in which our interests coincide. This is a good foundation for the further development of the Leninist principle of peaceful coexistence in international relations.

The powerful upsurge in the antiwar movement, which has embraced the entire globe, has become the sign of the times. Lenin's words serve as a warning: "The war is terrible; it has hit the vast mass of the people hardest of all...." The slogan "No to war!" is spreading throughout Europe, and is echoed in the United States and heard the world over.

The antiwar movement has become an influential factor in international life. The ruling circles in the United States and the other NATO countries have to take into account public protests against the arms race and against the deployment of U.S. missiles in

Western Europe. These protests reflect a new level of social consciousness and activity among the masses.

Communists and Social Democrats, Christians and Liberals,
trade union, religious, women's, youth, and other organizations
approach the struggle for peace from largely different political and
ideological positions. But they have a common goal: to prevent the
catastrophe which the warmongers are preparing for mankind. The
conviction that this goal can be attained is growing ever stronger.
War can and must be prevented.

Our comrades, the Communists, are in the front ranks of the
fighters against war. The Communist and workers' parties are
fighting a selfless battle to avert a thermonuclear war; they promote
the struggle waged by the masses against the threat of war, and point
correctly to imperialism as its social source.

We regard with approval the antiwar, anti-imperialist, and anti-
colonialist trend in the Nonalignment Movement, which was confirmed at the conference in Delhi. People in the liberated countries
are relating more and more clearly that it is possible to achieve
complete political and economic independence, build up their
national economies, and restructure international economic relations on a democratic basis only in close connection with the
struggle against the arms race and the war threat.

We note with satisfaction that our peace initiatives are in accord
with the ideas of our friends and are winning their support. Members of Communist, revolutionary-democratic, national-patriotic
and other parties spoke of this during the celebration of the sixtieth
anniversary of the Soviet Union, and the broad approval of the
proposals made in Prague by the Political Consultative Committee
of the Warsaw Treaty also testifies to this support.

Our country regards as its historic responsibility the building
of an impregnable barrier on the road of imperialism's inhumane
course. We are motivated by a concern not only for the security of
the Soviet people and of the fraternal peoples in the socialist
countries, but also for the future of civilization as a whole. The
strengthening of peace is the lodestar pointing the way to the future
of international relations. The Soviet Union stands for the elimination of tension in the international situation, for normal, good

relations with all states, including the United States of America.

We base ourselves on the fundamental conclusion drawn by the 26th Party Congress: No task is more important today for our party on an international plane than to safeguard peace. As loyal Leninists we shall spare no effort to win victory for the cause of peace, to secure a peaceful future for mankind.

April 22, 1983

4

CREATIVE EFFORT
OF THE PEOPLE

SOCIALISM has been exerting and continues to exert the most important influence on world development through its economic policy, through its achievements in the social and economic field. Each step forward along this road is the most convincing argument in favor of the socialist system and the Soviet way of life.

Socialism needs no justification for its existence; it is a natural product of social development. A new society has an enormous power of attraction, but this attraction hardly means that we can afford, even for a minute, to relax our attention on the popularization of its achievements, advantages, ideology, and morality. Our party's experience proves how great is the influence exerted on man's consciousness by truthful statements, irrefutable facts, and vivid images. Socialist ideology brings with it the truly humanistic ideals of social progress, development of the individual, of a world without weapons and wars, without exploitation and oppression.

It is not we but capitalism that has to maneuver and put on masks, resort to wars and terror, falsification and sabotage in order to hold back the implacable onslaught of time. Herein lie the origins of the global confrontation between the two systems on an increasingly broader front and of the continuing attempts of social revanchism, the plans for which are being hatched by the imperialist ruling circles. The stockpiling of arms and the whipping up of militarism, both material and psychological, and preparations for nuclear war are actually an admission by capitalism of the fact that it has exhausted its historical potential. The general crisis of capitalism means not only the aggravation of its economic, social and political contradictions. It also means a spiritual crisis, an ideological and moral crisis.

Capitalism has no future. And it is no accident that social development as depicted by capitalist ideologists has come to a dead end and is frozen, as it were. Herein lies not only ideological and

---

This speech was included in the book because of its significance.

theoretical impotence, but also a grave practical danger. A system which has no future fails to value either the past or the present. Herein lies the root cause of adventuristic imperialist policy.

The driving forces behind the current turn in international politics are multifarious. This turn is based on the continuing general crisis of capitalism. Its aggravation in the late 1970s and early 1980s undermined noticeably the whole fabric of economic and political relations in the capitalist world that had been established in the postwar period. In the center of the objective changes was the gradual yet increasingly apparent loss by the United States of its former economic and political domination and the erosion of its positions as compared with the new "centers of force," primarily Western Europe and Japan. U.S. imperialism was trying to resolve its own contradictions both at the expense of socialism and the developing countries and at the expense of its capitalist partners, and to make the latter more obedient to its will both economically and politically.

The sinister influence of the military-industrial complex has become noticeably predominant. This complex is playing an increasingly greater role in the policies of the leading capitalist states. Multinational capital, which seeks to prevent the new countries and peoples from embarking on the road of noncapitalist development and to keep new states in the capitalist orbit, also adds to the whipping up of confrontation. The military-strategic parity between the Soviet Union and the United States and the steady consolidation of the peace-loving foreign policy of the socialist community are coming into increasingly greater conflict with the aggressive strategic designs of imperialists.

It was under these circumstances that imperialism adopted a policy of undermining détente, stepping up the confrontation with socialism, whipping up the arms race, and fanning "psychological warfare." However, this reckless policy in world affairs is now spearheaded not only against socialism and other forces of democracy, progress, and national liberation. Imperialism, pinning its hopes on a military solution to the historical dispute between the two social systems, sets itself against the vital interests of all nations.

The declared "crusade" against communism is not only rhetoric, not only abuse of which Washington's politicians are so fond. It implies far-reaching hegemonistic ambitions. The intent of the "twentieth-century crusaders" is to ensure the attainment of global economic, political, and military-strategic objectives of imperialism, first and foremost, U.S. imperialism.

We are witnessing attempts to subordinate world economic ties, trade, credit, and financial relations to the selfish interests of American monopolies. By increasing interest rates artificially, these monopolies recently have been attracting up to 100 billion dollars of foreign capital a year to finance their activities. At the same time, the latest estimates show that the total direct capital investments by American business in foreign enterprises have topped 260 billion dollars, while their manufactured goods are said to cost more than a trillion dollars. All these factors exert a destabilizing influence on the economies of the United States' partners.

The United States ensnares many developing countries in its economic net. By penetrating their economies and sucking their lifeblood, the United States dooms such countries to prolonged backwardness and economic and political dependence. Bank loans at high interest rates are aimed at keeping the young states in bondage. Imperialism is directly responsible for the starvation and poverty of millions of people in the developing countries.

Economic expansion is accompanied by political and military aggression. What imperialism is doing in Nicaragua and El Salvador, in the Middle East, in Afghanistan, and in the south of Africa is nothing but state terrorism, the most flagrant violation of international law, and a manifestation of modern neocolonialism.

Imperialism's policy is inseparable from its ideology. This unity is determined by the interests of the class standing behind it. The ideological activity of the monopoly bourgeoisie has increased sharply over the past few years. Our opponent has developed a huge propaganda machine for ideological confrontation and is using highly sophisticated technology, means of subversion, and psychological ploys. By its intensity, content, and methods, the "psychological warfare" unleashed by imperialism constitutes a special type of aggression which tramples underfoot the sovereignty of other countries.

Posing as champions of humanism and human rights, capitalist ideologists are trying to impose on the socialist world norms and standards of a way of life that is alien to us and to undermine the lofty humanistic ideals without which man's work and life itself would be meaningless. They would like to cultivate among us customs and tastes predominant in bourgeois society, to "soften up" people's minds and make them susceptible to petty bourgeoisie ideas and petty, hollow temptations, to individualism, philistine fortune-hunting, ideological and cultural omnivorousness.

Under these circumstances, more than ever before, we need a principled party attitude, a consistent class approach to assessing current events and phenomena, political vigilance, intolerance of views which are alien to us, the creative and impelling nature of ideological work, efficiency, courage and perseverance. It is necessary to actively draw our scientists and specialists and professional people into information and propaganda work, not to be afraid of searching or experimenting, and to resolutely remove what has become outdated.

The active nature of our ideology consists not only in debunking bourgeois ideological myths and stereotypes. It is, above all, the assertion of our ideals, the socialist standards of public life, genuine freedom and democracy, and the story of our historical path. We all know that a new life does not come about by itself. It is necessary to fight for it perseveringly and selflessly, without shirking difficulties, without retreating after temporary setbacks.

Socialism was not built in a vacuum. We were compelled to overcome the fierce resistance of domestic and foreign reactionaries; the burden of people's age-old beliefs, prejudices, and habits; backwardness and ruin. Attempts were made to bring us to our knees economically and to destroy us physically. We were subjected to malicious persecution. We had our miscalculations, setbacks, and mistakes. For different reasons we have not managed to accomplish everything in the form, within the time limits, and with the results we would have liked to achieve. But we have scored great victories and achieved enormous heights of social progress.

Hence the need to develop in Soviet people, especially the younger generation, a clear understanding of the fact that it is impossible not only to move ahead, but also to preserve what has been gained without work, without struggle, without the complete dedication of each and every individual. Of course, life itself teaches people this truth. However, it would be dangerous in propaganda work to slide into the pattern of glossing over our reality.

New generations of Soviet people born under socialism are now entering active life. These are people to whom the historic gains of our system are as natural and inalienable as the air we breathe. Soviet young people are growing up and being educated in continuously improving material conditions over a period of four decades of peace. They are accustomed to comparing our reality no longer with the past, but with the highest criteria of socialism. And this perception constitutes one of the most important aspects of the present ideological situation. We must not let it slip from our view. It is our common concern to rear young people to make them ready for work and defense, to train them perseveringly in modern military skills, and to educate them in the spirit of love for our army and loyalty to military duty.

The active nature of our ideology lies in vigorous propaganda of the peace-loving foreign policy of the CPSU and the Soviet state as well as of the other countries in the socialist community. At a time when international tension has become seriously aggravated, the Central Committee of the party and the Soviet Government, together with the fraternal socialist countries, are doing everything to preserve and consolidate peace and prevent the threat of nuclear war. In this work, socialism sees its duty to world civilization.

What stands behind such phenomena as detente and the military-strategic parity between the Soviet Union and the United States is the intense labor of millions of people in the Soviet Union and the other socialist countries, their enormous economic might. Socialism does not need war, but no one should have any doubt that we will be able to defend our gains. The Soviet Union will continue to press for a constructive dialogue and for practical measures leading to a relaxation of international tension, to the establishment of an atmosphere of cooperation and mutual understanding among all nations.

December 10, 1984

5

SPEECH
IN THE
BRITISH PARLIAMENT

Ⅰ T IS with keen interest that we are getting acquainted with your country, its rich history and ancient culture, its diverse traditions formed in the course of many centuries, and with your hard-working and talented people who have given the world many outstanding thinkers, scholars, writers, and artists who are well known in the Soviet Union.

The Soviet people remember the ties between our peoples in the most devastating war of all time. They also remember how more than forty years ago a British prime minister presented the people of Stalingrad with an honorary sword, a symbol of close cooperation between the Soviet and British people in the anti-Hitler coalition.

In other words, we think that all the good, fruitful, and constructive things that our countries and peoples have acquired and accumulated in their relations over various historical periods should be preserved carefully and carried on.

It is almost ten years since a delegation of the Soviet Union's Supreme Soviet last came here. Serious changes have occurred since then in Soviet-British relations and in the international situation. This makes all the more apparent the need for such meetings as we are having today.

Hardly anyone will dispute that the destiny of Europe was indivisible—both when it lived in peace and concord and when storm clouds loomed over it. We have come to your country with the intention to discuss what can be done by our countries and parliaments to improve Soviet-British relations and the international situation in general. The future of mankind and relations between individual states and groups of states depend on the actions and concrete moves which are being or can be undertaken today on matters of war and peace and international cooperation.

These very issues were at the focus of our discussions with your Prime Minister, Mrs. Thatcher, the Secretary of State for

---

The excerpt from this speech was also included in the book because of its significance.

Foreign and Commonwealth Affairs, Sir Geoffrey Howe, and with other cabinet members. We think that our exchange of opinions was businesslike, frank, and fruitful. So, now in addressing the members of the British Parliament, we would first of all like to outline our views we find important for improvement of the international situation and for development of bilateral relations.

It is common knowledge that in the 1970s Europe became a cradle for the policy of detente. Important areas of cooperation between the countries of Western Europe, the Soviet Union, and other socialist countries were defined at that time. That process was then joined by the United States and Canada, which also signed the Final Act of the Helsinki Conference.

At one time the world managed to block the channels of further proliferation of nuclear weapons. That success was formalized in the international Treaty on the Non-Proliferation of Nuclear Weapons, signed to date by more than a hundred countries. Nuclear weapons tests in the atmosphere, outer space and underwater were stopped and banned, talks began on a complete and universal ban on such tests. As a result of Soviet-American agreements, certain restrictions were imposed in the field of strategic nuclear armaments and antiballistic-missile defense systems. An active search got under way for opportunities to curb the arms race in other areas too, involving both mass destruction weapons and conventional armaments. Political dialogue was gradually gathering momentum. There was a noticeable intensification in trade links, cultural, scientific, and other contacts. No one can dispute the obvious fact that in the years of detente life became more tranquil and their people came to have greater confidence in the future.

In short, it was a period when the international climate became healthier. It was not a case of concessions by one side to another. Rather, it was a case of realism based on proper regard for the individual interests of countries with different social systems, and of a general understanding that one cannot build his own security by impairing the security of others.

In other words, reason and realization of the fact that war is a wrong and unacceptable method of resolving disputes and that it is impossible to win in a nuclear war just as it is impossible to win in the arms race or in confrontation got the upper hand. It became obvious that the Cold War was an abnormal state of relations fraught constantly with danger of war. All that formed a foundation for the favorable course of international developments in the 1970s. On that foundation, peaceful coexistence between states with different social systems took ever deeper and stronger roots in the whole system of international affairs. We still believe that there is and can be no rational alternative to the policy of peaceful coexistence, and I would like to emphasize this point with all certainty.

The natural question arising from what I have said is why the danger of war forced back at the time has drawn closer once again. I would not like to go into details now. The Soviet view on this point is well known. Nevertheless, I would like to repeat that the turn for the worse — and this is confirmed by the facts — was caused by the changes in the policies of certain forces which have been trying to gain military superiority and thereby gain an opportunity to dictate their will to others.

The Soviet Union remembers perfectly the particular words and deeds which created the climate of mistrust and hostility and destabilized the international situation, but it is not to pique anyone that I am reminding you about that today.

We see our goal in joint settlement — since no one is in a position to do it single-handedly — of the more important problems which are essentially common to us. These are preventing war; stopping the arms race and proceeding to disarmament; settling existing and averting potential conflicts and crises; creating an international atmosphere and resources to settle one's own problems (show me a country which has no such problems); and pooling efforts in tackling such global problems as fighting famine and disease, protecting the environment, and providing mankind with energy and raw materials.

If Britain adheres to this line, we will be glad to cooperate with it. And if the United States stick to this line, too, and really puts its policy on the track of peaceful cooperation, it will find a reliable partner in us.

This is how we see the situation, and these are the views with which our parliamentary delegation has come to Britain.

If we agree with the initial premises which I have just spoken of, the main questions still remain: how to resolve the problems which all of us consider to be important, how to prevent the further development of the present dangerous situation and achieve a stable and reliable situation in the world. How can we overcome tension and the consequences of the Cold War and switch over again to détente, fruitful talks and cooperation?

Not only words are needed, though words are certainly important. Concrete deeds are needed. As a matter of fact, this task requires practical resolution of the existing problems. As we understand, now, more than ever before, it is important for each country, for its government, parliament, and political and public quarters to realize their responsibility for the state of affairs in the world. We in the Soviet Union retain memories of the horrors of the past war and are well aware what a future war may result in, and we have been doing and continue to do everything in our power to live up to this high responsibility.

I am not going to enumerate all our foreign-policy proposals and initiatives here. I want only to say that they envisage the most radical reduction in nuclear weapons (with a view to eventually scrapping them completely) as well as conventional armaments and the prohibition of chemical weapons and elimination of their stockpiles. We would like to hold a broad dialogue and to develop equal and mutually advantageous cooperation in resolving the pressing political problems, and those in the economic sphere, in science and technology, and in the promotion of cultural relations and exchanges.

When we speak about war and peace, we must bear in mind that the nature of present-day armaments, and especially nuclear ones, has changed the traditional notion of these problems. Mankind is now on the threshold of a new stage in the scientific and technological revolution which is bound to tell on the further development of military technology. Those who engage in phrase-mongering about "limited," "lightning," or "protracted" nuclear wars evidently remain prisoners of the outdated stereotypes characteristic of the time when a war was a great evil but, unlike today, did not threaten all humankind with annihilation. The nuclear age inevitably dictates new political thinking. Preventing a nuclear war is the most burning issue for all people on earth.

Our proposal to establish certain norms of conduct for the nuclear powers is aimed at removing the threat of a nuclear war, finding a way to stop the arms race, and bringing about such a situation in the world in which people would have no fear for tomorrow. It is also relevant to say here that the Soviet Union has already assumed unilaterally an obligation not to be the first to use nuclear weapons.

This is our fundamental line, and we proceed from these ideas in all our proposals aimed at curbing the arms race and preventing war.

Guided by this, the Soviet Union has recently advanced an initiative for holding talks with the United States on a package of issues concerning nuclear and space armaments. On the basis of this initiative, an agreement has been reached with the U.S. administration to start entirely new talks which would embrace the question of nonmilitarization of space and the questions of reducing nuclear arms, both strategic and medium-range. All these questions are to be considered and resolved in their interconnection. Of key importance in all this discussion is prevention of a space arms race. Such a race would not only be dangerous in itself; it would give a boost to the arms race in other areas. The Soviet Union is prepared to seek and work out the most radical measures on all these issues, measures which would help advance toward complete prohibition and eventual elimination of nuclear weapons. It is now up to the United States to make a move, to take this time a realistic stand which would make for effective negotiations.

We know that everything relating to the reduction of the nuclear danger is being widely discussed in Great Britain and other countries in Western Europe. It goes without saying that the questions of defense and security must be decided by sovereign states themselves. However, I might state that any concrete step toward removing the threat of a nuclear war anywhere – including Europe – will find a corresponding practical response on our part.

It is true, of course, that not infrequently the stands of the Soviet Union and Great Britain on crucial international matters differ. Neither we nor you would hide this fact. But it is our deep conviction that at the present time, more than ever before, all countries and peoples need constructive dialogue and a search for solutions to the key international issues; spheres of accord have to be found which would promote confidence among countries and create such an atmosphere in international relations as would be free from a nuclear threat, hostility, suspicion, fear, and enmity.

My country set forth its attitude in plain and unambiguous terms: Tension should be overcome and disagreements and disputes resolved at the negotiating table, with due consideration for each side's legitimate interests, and not by means of threat or use of force, and interference in internal affairs should be excluded. We all must learn to live together, proceeding from the realities of our contemporary world, which is changing constantly, following its own laws.

The development of the world situation is affected greatly by the way in which relations between the European countries are shaped. I have already said that such relations were particularly favorable in the 1970s, especially following the adoption of the Final Act of the Helsinki Conference on Security and Cooperation in Europe. This document remains a life-giving source sustaining the trends toward mutual understanding and cooperation in Europe and beyond. We feel it essential to protect this source and not to allow it to be discredited.

To a great extent, good relations among European countries are a guarantee of world tranquility and peace. The peoples of our continent paid dearly for realizing that under no circumstances shall they indulge the forces which have not given up attempts to change the territorial realities which have taken shape in Europe after the Second World War. These realities are the fruit of our common victory. They have been reflected and sealed in the Allied agreements on the postwar European arrangement, in major bilateral treaties, and in the Helsinki Final Act. Adherence to these documents would be a firm obstacle in the way of those who would like to call into question the results of the Second World War, postwar developments, and the inviolability of frontiers in Europe. There should be no ambiguity on this score.

The Stockholm Conference could open up prospects for a more

secure peace in Europe. An important proposal concerning a treaty on not using armed force and on the maintenance of peace was submitted to the conference. We believe that major political and international legal steps, backed by confidence-building measures in the military field in pursuance of the Helsinki Final Act, would make the Stockholm Conference a success and its results a weighty contribution to the strengthening of security in Europe and elsewhere.

I have dwelt on some of the more pressing issues, whose resolution would help stop the arms race and promote security on a European and world scale. I would like to stress once again that the Soviet leadership stands for forthright and honest talks which would help us to advance, on a mutually acceptable basis, in the solution of the question of limiting and reducing weapons — primarily nuclear weapons — and finally eliminating them completely. We are ready to go as far as our Western partners do. Naturally enough, equality and equal security shall underlie any agreements in this field, and, naturally, any course aimed at the achievement of military superiority over the Soviet Union and its allies is unacceptable and has no prospects.

We all agree that ours is a vulnerable, rather fragile, yet interdependent world where we must coexist whether we want to or not. For all that separates us, we have one planet, and Europe is our common home, not a "theater of operations."

The Soviet Union is in favor of better relations among nations. In politics and diplomacy there is always room for reasonable compromises, and a vast field for the development and strengthening of mutual understanding and trust on the basis of similar or mutual interests. All that is needed is to work for these goals. The Soviet Union and Britain, the Soviet and British peoples, do have coinciding interests, with peace being the foremost one.

Going back over sixty years, the history of Soviet-British relations contains unforgettable landmarks. Since the war we have seen years of fruitful cooperation, but these were also years of slump. Nowadays the relations between our countries, which are developing not in a political vacuum, but in an atmosphere permeated with the growing danger of a nuclear war, are not on the upgrade and are far from what can be desired. I want to remind you that at one time Britain ranked first in trade with the Soviet Union. It has now gone to seventh or eight place. I agree with those British businessmen and industrialists who say that politics should promote trade, which, in turn, should facilitate mutual understanding and strengthen confidence. And this is as it should be.

December 18, 1984

6

MEETING WITH REPRESENTATIVES OF THE BRITISH BUSINESS WORLD

O<small>N</small> DECEMBER 20, 1984, the delegation of the Supreme Soviet of the USSR, on an official visit to Great Britain, met the leading officials of the London Chamber of Commerce and Industry, the British-Soviet Chamber of Commerce and the Confederation of British Industry. The delegation was headed by Mikhail Gorbachev, member of the Politburo and Secretary of the CPSU Central Committee and Chairman of the Commission on Foreign Affairs of the USSR Supreme Soviet. Present at the meeting were top British industrialists and heads of trade, commercial and financial organizations. Mikhail Gorbachev addressed the audience with the following speech.

*　　*　　*

The organizations you are in charge of and many of the industrial and commercial companies and banks represented here are well known in the Soviet Union as reliable partners in Anglo-Soviet trade and economic as well as scientific and technological relations, as partisans of good traditions of long standing in what is an important area for our nations and peoples.

Our delegation has come to Great Britain to meet our colleagues, British members of Parliament, as well as other political and state figures, and to exchange views on current international problems, first of all, on the ways of easing international tension, and on questions of Soviet-British bilateral relations.

We had a useful and, in our opinion, a very topical discussion with the Prime Minister of Great Britain, Mrs. Margaret Thatcher. In the part of the discussion that dealt with bilateral relations, we were of the same view, that it is necessary to steer Anglo-Soviet relations onto a new, positive course. This is relevant to trade and economic relations as well. Freezing the relations between the Soviet Union and Great Britain, as experience has shown, does not lead to anything good. Neither you nor we benefit from this course.

I would like to emphasize that this was one of the main ideas contained in the message of the head of our state and party, Konstantin Chernenko, to the Prime Minister of Great Britain.

The last sixty years have seen quite a few examples of positive fruitful cooperation.

I think you will agree with me if I say that it is very important to promote traditions of this kind and to strengthen cooperation and mutual understanding at so involved and crucial a moment for Europe and the world. I am sure I am not alone in the conviction that the European public and the entire world community are, literally with every day, increasingly sensitive to the growing tension and, I would say, to the incongruity of the present international situation with the objective interests of humanity and, indeed, with the requirements of the nuclear age.

As to the Soviet Union, it is working for the threat of nuclear war to be averted, for the arms race to be stopped, and for a climate of confidence to be created between all nations and peoples. The main thing today is to avert a nuclear disaster. The Soviet Union has recently proposed to the U.S. the opening of fresh negotiations to cover the whole set of issues relating to prevention of the militarization of outer space and reductions in strategic nuclear arms and medium-range nuclear weapons. We are ready to work out the most radical solutions with regard to all of these issues.

To carry out these and our other proposals aimed at the removal of the nuclear threat, the West and, above all, the United States of America must meet us halfway. It yet remains to be seen whether the U.S. administration will adopt a really constructive approach this time.

As Konstantin Chernenko, the Soviet head of state, said in his address to the British readers in his book, which has recently been published in Great Britain, "The British and, indeed, all people on Earth may rest assured that the USSR will honestly and constructively cooperate with all states prepared to help lessen international tension by practical steps and create an atmosphere of trust in the world."

I would like to add that in his message to Mrs. Margaret Thatcher it was said openly that the Soviet Union will remain devoted to the aims and ways of peaceful cooperation among

European states. Precisely on this platform we have been building and will continue to build our foreign policy.

The efforts of all nations large and small, of all peoples, are required in the struggle for peace and for prevention of a nuclear war. No one in the modern, highly tense world can afford to stay out of the struggle to prevent war.

At this meeting of ours I would like to stress in particular the increased political role of business links. The very course of life has proved that it is impossible to create a material base for strengthening and extending détente without well-established and stable international economic relations. It is this understanding, as well as realism in politics, that has made it possible to work out a program that found its expression in the most important political document of the postwar period—the Final Act of the Helsinki Conference.

How do we see international economic relations? We have repeatedly spoken on that issue. At their economic summit conference last summer, the member countries of the Council for Mutual Economic Assistance stressed the need to honor the assumed commitments in the process of international economic relations, to end discrimination, and not to allow economic instruments to be used as means a political pressure and intervention in the internal affairs of sovereign states. You will agree with me that the application of these principles is certainly conducive to normal and business relations. Relations on such a basis would benefit everyone and benefit them significantly.

In promoting economic cooperation, the partners concerned want to know as much as possible about each other. Businessmen have more confidence in facts and figures than in any words, and that is quite natural. As for the Soviet Union, I am going to give you some facts regarding its economic, scientific, and technological potential.

As this juncture, the USSR is producing one-fifth of the world's industrial output.

I shall not elaborate on all the branches where the Soviet Union is the world's top producer. Nevertheless, I shall say that they cover mineral extraction, energy production, including nuclear energy, a wide range of machine-building, and many others.

Here is just one figure to illustrate the dynamics of Soviet economic growth: The volume of industrial output under the present five-year plan (1981-1985) is greater than in the three prewar five-year plans put together.

A full-scale effort is under way to draft the guidelines for national economic and social development for 1986-1990 and for a longer period, up to the end of the century. How do we see these programs? The job has yet to be completed, but even at this point it is possible to speak of the fundamental directions. To put it in a nutshell, these will be years of further stable growth rates and dynamic progress in all sectors of the national economy, years of further improvement in the material well-being of the Soviet people.

We are sure of our ability to resolve by ourselves whatever problems may arise in our economy. However, we naturally do not rule out the possibility for the broadest possible cooperation with foreign firms, including British companies.

It is no longer possible for any nation or group of nations to have a monopoly on scientific and technological achievements. Broad-scale international cooperation is needed, and, in our view, possibilities for that do exist. We need more realism and trust in each other, gentlemen!

Our plans are reliable landmarks for all those who want to cooperate with the Soviet Union. I would like to note in this context that these plans will place substantial emphasis on the Soviet Union's external economic ties. "Capitalist states," as head of our state Konstantin Chernenko has emphasized, "must know that, given respect for the principle of mutual benefit, they will always find in the Soviet Union an honest and well-wishing partner willing to promote cooperation on the basis of equality and mutual advantage."

Now I would like to touch upon the current state of Soviet-British trade and economic relations. Their record is not simple for there have been ups and downs and serious complications as well as periods of vigor. The general trend in business cooperation between our countries came through in the latter half of the 1970s, when the atmosphere of détente made for wider and stronger mutually beneficial economic ties between states with different social systems. Let me mention the 1974 Agreement on the Development of Economic, Scientific, Technological and Industrial Cooperation and the 1975 Long-Term Program for the Development of Economic and Industrial Cooperation, which have defined the main areas of our ties for a considerable period.

Soviet foreign trade organizations and a number of British companies — John Brown, ICI, Shell and Courtaulds — have entered into long-term agreements, while the total number of British companies involved in trade with the USSR now exceeds 1,500. All this suggests that Soviet-British trade and economic relations can develop on a large scale and, of course, to the mutual advantage of both countries.

While positively assessing the experience accumulated, one cannot avoid mentioning problems and difficulties as well. Quantitative restrictions still remain on exports to Great Britain of a number of Soviet goods. We see so-called antidumping procedures being applied against our traditional export commodities. The terms for financing British exports to the USSR have worsened. We have always stressed that the various artificial restrictions in foreign economic ties do not benefit trading partners and run counter to the long-term interests of cooperation. I presume you also share that view.

I regard it necessary to underscore the important role of the permanent Soviet-British Inter-Governmental Commission for Cooperation in the Fields of Applied Science, Technology, Trade and Economic Relations in promoting mutually beneficial cooperation. While discussing the problems of Soviet-British trade and economic relations with Mrs. Thatcher, we have come to the conclusion that they must be enhanced, and significantly. The Commission must also have its say here.

I won't be wrong if I say that most of the British business world's representatives in this audience welcome a considerable broadening of our trade. We think that this is quite realistic. For instance, talks are presently under way for orders by the Soviet Union of British machinery and equipment to the tune of hundreds of millions of rubles.

In a talk with Mrs. Thatcher I said that, in my opinion, the trade turnover between our countries could be increased in the near future by 40 to 50 percent.

An opportunity is opening up for British firms to participate in the construction or reconstruction of plants in the automobile, chemical, oil, gas, food and light industries, ferrous and non-ferrous metallurgy, mechanical engineering, as well as in projects envisaged under the Food Program of the USSR for the period up to 1990.

In October 1984 British companies were invited to participate in the building of two large chemical complexes in the USSR to produce polyester fibres and propylolefines. The overall cost of these projects is tentatively put at a very solid sum.

The head of the delegation said that when visiting the ICI company, the Soviet side asked the heads of the firm to think over the idea of designing, building, and completely equipping a complex enterprise in the Soviet Union for the production of certain types of herbicides and pesticides which are necessary in order to introduce intensive technological methods into farming.

I would like to note that great opportunities in this context are opening up not only for large, but also for medium-sized and small British firms, and I intentionally stress this. Of course, the success of British firms on the Soviet market will depend on the competitiveness of their offers, on how timely these will be and on the terms of financing.

We proceed from the premise that a stable and ongoing situation is essential for trade and economic cooperation and that an atmosphere must be created that would favor this process. It is no secret that some Western quarters are all too ready to present the readiness of the Soviet Union to participate in this process as almost a sign of "weakness" on its part. The opponents of "economic détente"—and they, unfortunately, are still to be found in the world—are trying to turn trade with the USSR and other socialist countries into a tool for political pressure.

We also hear assertions that purchases of Western licenses and patents ensure the Soviet Union access to the latest technology, which, allegedly, it would not be in a position to develop on its own.

This is a deeply erroneous point of view. And we have on many occasions proved just the opposite.

The achievements of the Soviet Union in fundamental and applied sciences have won recognition throughout the world. Today the USSR is capable of independently tackling the most complex scientific and technological tasks.

I think the thesis that East-West trade benefits only the socialist countries is equally groundless. The businessmen present in this hall know perfectly well that trade can only be reciprocally advantageous. It has been known since ancient times that without mutual benefit you can't strike a deal. Now, too, no party will agree to trade to its own disadvantage.

Discrimination in trade does harm primarily to those who engender it because it turns into a loss of lucrative orders for them.

The British business community must also have noticed this. As a result of the policy I mentioned above, trade between the USSR and Great Britain had shrunk by almost 20 percent by 1982 compared with 1979. Only this year it is expected that our trade turnover will return to the 1979 level. Great Britain, once one of the main trade partners of the USSR, in 1983 ranked seventh among the USSR's trading partners from the industrialized capitalist states, and in 1982 it had been ninth.

The policy of embargoes and sanctions used by someone from time to time is, frankly speaking, directed not only against the socialist countries; it also seeks to weaken competitors, West European ones included. We pay tribute to the efforts of the British firms that, despite certain pressure, have been guided by common sense, commercial interests, and the trade traditions of your country, and continue to honor their obligations in trade with the Soviet Union.

In conclusion, I would like to emphasize the thought with which I began my speech, that the development of Soviet-British ties will help improve the general political climate and create an atmosphere of trust and constructive cooperation between the East and the West as a whole.

You in Great Britain say: "Rain before seven, fine before eleven." This proverb expresses the optimism intrinsic to your people. Neither are we pessimists by nature. But, nevertheless, with all the optimism one shouldn't hope that fine weather in relations between countries will come by itself, without mutual efforts.

*   *   *

Mikhail Gorbachev expressed the gratitude of the Soviet delegation for the attention and hospitality accorded them.

7

A MEETING ON
DISARMAMENT

O<small>N</small> MARCH 22, 1985 Mikhail Gorbachev, General Secretary of the CPSU Central Committee, met in the Kremlin with members of the Advisory Council on Disarmament of the Socialist International.

Kalevi Sorsa, Vice President of the Socialist International and Chairman of the Advisory Council on Disarmament, congratulated Mikhail Gorbachev on his election as General Secretary of the CPSU Central Committee. Sorsa told about the activities of the Council for Limitation and Discontinuation of the Arms Race. The parties in the Socialist International are concerned about the situation in the world, especially the incessant arms buildup. The Advisory Council of the Socialist International opposes, in particular, the militarization of outer space. The hope was expressed that the Soviet Union and the United States would make every effort to curb the arms race and to end it altogether. Sorsa said that the Soviet Union and the United States would make every effort to curb the arms race and to end it altogether. Sorsa said that the Socialist and Social-Democratic Parties in the Socialist International would work toward that goal. Noting that the limitation of the arms race was a problem that affected not only the Soviet Union and the United States, but all of mankind, he said that small countries and neutral and nonaligned states also could and should contribute to the cause.

Mikhail Gorbachev stressed that the foreign policy of the CPSU and the Soviet state remained unchanged, as the March 1985 Plenary Meeting of the CPSU Central Committee had confirmed. The Soviet Union would follow unswervingly a course of peace and progress.

It was noted during the meeting that an alarming situation had arisen in the world.

* * *

The threat of nuclear war continues to grow. The arms race, if not curbed now, could enter a qualitatively new phase in which uncontrollable processes would begin. The situation is complicated further by deliberate actions to undermine international trust and to step up confrontation in every sphere. Threats of armed force and open intervention in the affairs of independent states are resorted to merely because the realities of today's world do not suit certain people.

The peace-loving public of the entire world calls for an end to the dangerous arms race and removal of the threat of war. Great hopes in this respect are pinned on the new Soviet-American talks started recently in Geneva.

It is of primary significance that the objective of the talks, as set down in the joint Soviet-American statement, will be the working out of effective accords aimed at preventing an arms race in outer space and ending the one on earth, at limiting and reducing nuclear armaments, and strengthening strategic stability. In the final analysis, the sides agreed, the talks are intended to bring about the elimination of all nuclear weapons everywhere.

Progress in the Geneva talks and their fruitfulness, Mikhail Gorbachev stressed, depend on whether both sides will abide strictly by all parts of their agreement on the subject and aims of the talks. The Soviet Union will do everything in its power to fulfill this agreement and will judge the intentions of the American side by its actions. It is essential that each side should show goodwill and readiness for reasonable compromises, and most important of all, that the principles of equality and equal security should be observed strictly.

We are resolutely against the talks being turned into a kind of cover for continued escalation of the arms race, said Mikhail Gorbachev. That is why the Soviet Union proposes a freeze on the sides' nuclear arsenals and an end to the further deployment of missiles. Among other things we are convinced that an end to the deployment of new U.S. missiles in Europe with a simultaneous end to the implementation of soviet countermeasures would help resolve substantially the entire range of issues under discussion in Geneva.

The efforts of the most diverse public and political forces of our time are directed toward preventing nuclear war. Such is the aim of the major peace initiatives put forward by the Soviet Union and other countries of the socialist community. These initiatives are in accord with the UN resolutions that reflect the views of the world community. The public and leaders of many countries have been speaking out unequivocally for a return to détente, an end to the arms race, and the development of political dialogue and coopera- tion between states. The antiwar movement, which has become a major sociopolitical force in many countries, advocates that goal emphatically. The awareness is spreading that in a nuclear age the security of states cannot be based on force or threat of force. Security is possible only when it is security for all. All this strength- ens the conviction that, given the necessary efforts, there can be a change in the situation, and improvement in the international cli- mate.

We know about the activities of the Advisory Council on Disarmament of the Socialist International and appreciate its efforts to promote constructive dialogue and negotiations, Mikhail Gorba- chev said. The parties of the Socialist International, considering their political leverage and influence, can help improve the interna- tional situation in many ways, bring about an end to the arms race, and increase their contribution to saving mankind from nuclear catastrophe. The international situation urgently demands energetic and effective efforts by the working-class and democratic move- ment in the struggle against the threat of war. The CPSU, for its part, is prepared to cooperate vigorously with all peace-loving public forces, including the parties in the Socialist International. This is our firm and invariable course, and we will continue to pursue it consistently.

8

INTERVIEW WITH
THE EDITOR OF *PRAVDA*

QUESTION: *Pravda* is getting many letters from readers at home and abroad on international affairs. How would you describe the present international situation?

Answer: I can understand the heightened interest of the people in international affairs. Broad masses of the people on all continents want to exert a definite influence on the future of our world.

This is not surprising. The world is full of complex problems— political, economic, and social. Two opposite social systems— socialism and capitalism—exist. This is a fact. Dozens of new states with their different histories, traditions and interests are active in the international arena. This, too, is a fact.

In building international relations in today's world, we cannot avoid taking this into account. We must not ignore the interests of other states or, what is more, try to deny them their right to choose their own path of development. In a broad sense, this is the policy of peaceful coexistence under which each of the systems will prove which is better by force of example and not by strength of arms.

Another conclusion, just as pertinent, is that it is necessary to stop the arms race. The international situation has reached the point where one has to ask: What other path lies ahead? Is it not high time for those who determine the policies of states to stop and think so as to avoid making decisions that might push the world toward a nuclear holocaust?

There is an acute need for international cooperation in establishing a dialogue and searching for realistic solutions that would ease tension in the world and help block the avenues of the arms race.

All countries, large and small, should take part in this goal. Understandably, a special role here belongs to the nuclear powers and, first of all, to the Soviet Union and the United States of America.

Our country has always pursued and will continue to pursue a vigorous and constructive foreign policy aimed at consolidating peace. This was confirmed at the recent plenary meeting of the

CPSU Central Committee at which the foreign-policy principles of the Soviet state were outlined.

Question: Much of the world depends on the state of Soviet-American relations. Do you think there are possibilities for their changing for the better?

Answer: Relations between the Soviet Union and the United States are an exceptionally important factor in international politics. But we hardly look at the world through the prism of those relations alone. We understand what role other countries have to play in international affairs and take this into consideration when evaluating the general situation in the world.

Are there any changes for the better in Soviet-American relations at the moment? There is no simple answer to this question. There is some reason for hope, but a great deal more that gives cause for alarm.

New Soviet-American talks on nuclear and space arms have begun in Geneva. This is a positive note. We defined the subject and aims of the talks jointly with the United States and briefly defined them as follows: not to start an arms race in space and to stop the arms race on earth and proceed toward a radical reduction in nuclear arms so as ultimately to do away with them altogether.

Now we have to carry out what we have agreed upon. The talks are important. I am saying this first of all because the direction for the further development of Soviet-American relations and for world development as a whole is now being decided. The choice is either an arms race in all spheres and the growing threat of war, or the strengthening of universal security and a more enduring peace for all.

There are some changes for the better in other areas of Soviet-American relations, but they are very small. On the whole, relations remain tense.

Washington relies on strength and makes no secret of it. And it is counting on gaining superiority in strength that would lead to the subordination of the rest of the world to America. For it, diplomacy and talks are literally subordinated to missiles and bombers. It is a fact that new strategic arms programs are being pushed through Congress by the same people who are conducting the talks in

Geneva on behalf of the United States.

Everybody has heard a great deal about the "Star Wars" plans announced by the United States administration. The terminology appears to be taken from science fiction, but it is used to hide a real and serious danger to our planet. I would describe as fantastic the arguments that are used to serve as a basis for the militarization of space. They talk about defense but prepare for attack. They advertise a space shield but are forging a space sword. They promise to liquidate nuclear armaments but in practice build up these armaments and improve them. They promise the world stability but in reality are working to disrupt the military equilibrium.

Since people intuitively sense the danger of the "Star Wars" plans, the authors of these plans want to make them believe that they amount to nothing more than harmless research, which, moreover, promises technological benefits. By dangling this bait, they want to turn their allies into accomplices in this dangerous venture.

It is even asserted that by creating space weapons it is possible to do away with nuclear arms. This is a trick to deceive people. Just as the emergence of nuclear weapons did not eliminate the conventional types of arms and only brought about the accelerated race in both nuclear and conventional arms, the creation of space weapons can have only one result: The arms race will become even more intensive and will embrace new spheres.

I have singled out those aspects which especially complicate Soviet-American relations, sometimes bringing them to the verge of acute tension. But it appears that there are people in the United States who regard such a state of affairs as normal and view confrontation as almost natural.

We do not think so. Confrontation is not an innate defect in our relations; it is an anomaly. It is not inevitable that it should be maintained. We consider an improvement in Soviet-American relations not only extremely necessary, but also possible. But, of course, reciprocity is required.

Question: There is a great deal of interest in the possibility of your meeting with the President of the United States. What are the prospects for a meeting?

Answer: The question of such a meeting has been touched upon in my correspondence with President Reagan. I can say that a positive attitude to such a meeting has been expressed on both sides. The time and place of this meeting will be fixed later.

On a broader plane, our correspondence touched upon the search for joint ways of improving relations between the Soviet Union and the United States and imparting a more stable and constructive character to them. I am convinced that a serious impetus should be given to the development of Soviet-American relations at a high political level. We propose to the Government of the United States that these matters should be conducted in such a way that all our peoples and other nations would see that the policies of the Soviet Union and the United States are oriented not toward hostility and confrontation, but toward a search for mutual understanding and peaceful development.

Question: From what you have said, it follows that work is needed in a wide range of fields. But still, what do you regard as the main lever for achieving a radical change for the better?

Answer: Intensive joint efforts. And, indeed, efforts in a wide range of fields. A mutual understanding of the need to facilitate the settlement of conflict situations in the world would have a beneficial influence on our relations and on international relations as a whole. A great deal can be done to mutual advantage through this development of bilateral ties between the Soviet Union and the United States.

But still, what you called the main lever lies in the sphere of security. In what way exactly can we make a start here?

If one has come to the negotiating table to discuss reductions in arms, one should at least refrain from building them up. That is why we propose that the Soviet Union and the United States introduce, for the entire duration of the talks, a moratorium on the development (including research), testing, and deployment of attack space weapons and a freeze on their strategic offensive arms. At the same time, the deployment of American medium-range missiles in Europe should be terminated and, correspondingly, the buildup of our countermeasures.

American leaders are declaring that they are for radical reductions in armaments. If that is so, it would be logical first to put a brake on the arms race and then to proceed immediately to arms reductions.

We are for honest dialogue. We are prepared to demonstrate our goodwill again. And, as of today—and I would like to emphasize this—the Soviet Union is introducing a moratorium on the deployment of its medium-range missiles and suspending other countermeasures in Europe. The moratorium will last until November of this year. The decision we shall make after that will depend on whether the United States follows our example: whether it will stop the deployment of its medium-range missiles in Europe.

To sum up, the opportunities for improving Soviet-American relations, for improving the international situation in general, do exist. These opportunities should not be missed. They should be translated into definite policies and practical measures.

April 8, 1985

9

MEETING WITH SPEAKER THOMAS O'NEILL

O N APRIL 10, 1985, General Secretary of the CPSU Central Committee Mikhail Gorbachev received Speaker of the House of Representatives of the U.S. Congress Thomas O'Neill, who headed a delegation from the House of Representatives on a visit to the Soviet Union at the invitation of the USSR Supreme Soviet. Mikhail Gorbachev and Thomas O'Neill held a conversation in the Kremlin attended by Chairman of the Soviet of the Union of the USSR Supreme Soviet Lev Tolkunov and members of the U.S. House of Representatives Robert Michel, Dan Rostenkowski, and Silvio Conte, and U.S. Ambassador to the Soviet Union Arthur Hartman.

*   *   *

Welcoming the American congressmen, Mikhail Gorbachev expressed satisfaction that the official delegation from the U.S. House of Representatives was having an active political dialogue with their colleagues from the USSR Supreme Soviet, which both sides assessed as positive.

We know the role played by Congress in America's political life, and we attach great importance to developing contacts along the parliamentary line as one of the elements of invigorating Soviet-American relations.

The times are such now that people shaping policy in the two countries should definitely converse with one another. The world situation is disquieting, even dangerous, and there is a kind of ice age in relations between the Soviet Union and the United States (at least, this was so until very recently.)

Mikhail Gorbachev emphasized that the Soviet leadership sincerely wishes that Soviet-American relations would return to normalcy. We do not think that behind present tensions in these relations is some fatal clash of national interests. On the contrary, our peoples can gain much from the development of broad and fruitful cooperation, to say nothing of the fact that they are united by

the dominating common interest of ensuring security and preserving the very life of our peoples. The difference in the social systems,
in the ideology of our countries is no cause for curtailing relations,
much less for kindling hatred.

Life shows that Soviet-American mutually beneficial cooperation is quite possible. A number of fundamental documents signed
by both sides in 1972 and 1973 laid the groundwork for fruitful
cooperation in various fields. This cooperation also contributed to
the extension of détente in international relations as a whole, in
particular to the success of the Helsinki Conference. In 1972 the
leaders of the Soviet Union and the United States put their signa-
tures to a document saying that peaceful coexistence between our
two countries is the only sensible alternative in this nuclear age.

This implies, of course, the recognition of the right of every
nation to arrange its life as it sees fit, without interference in its
internal affairs, without attempts to shape other countries according
to one's own fashion or to impose one's will on other people.

A genuine improvement in relations between the Soviet Union
and the United States requires political will by the leaders of both
countries. On the Soviet side, such a will exists. If it is displayed by
the American side as well, then many fundamental issues currently
separating our countries will gradually begin to be solved.

Mikhail Gorbachev dwelt in detail on matters of ensuring the
security of the people of both countries, of preventing nuclear war
and, in particular, on the Soviet-American talks in Geneva.

The Soviet Union agreed to the new talks with the United States
guided by a sense of profound responsibility to its people, to other
peoples for the cause of peace on earth. We are satisfied that the
United States accepted our proposal for talks. We agreed to them in
order to conduct them honestly and seriously, seeking to agree on
tangible, real results on very large reductions in strategic nuclear
weapons and medium-range weapons. But it is possible to attain
these objectives only if the American side gives up its provocative
designs for extending the arms race into outer space, where it wants
to secure the possibility of making a first nuclear strike with impunity under the cover of "defensive" weapons. That is why the
solution of the issues relating to ending the nuclear arms race on

earth and preventing it in outer space is a single problem that must be resolved in its entirety, as agreed upon by the Soviet Union and the United States in January of this year.

It is difficult to understand how one can tally statements by the United States on the intention to reach agreement on nuclear weapons reduction with the feverish everyday actions to build up these weapons. Claims made by the U.S. administration and propaganda that the Soviet Union enjoys a certain superiority in various types of nuclear weapons are an utter distortion of the fact. *(Mikhail Gorbachev cited facts and figures to show that, in reality, there is parity, or a rough balance between the Soviet Union and the NATO countries in all of these weapons.)* That is precisely why, wishing to fulfill the hopes of peoples, to reach the first specific results at the talks in Geneva and to ensure their further success, the Soviet Union has proposed a most natural and sensible solution: In the first place, put an end to a further buildup of the nuclear arsenals on earth, halt preparations for the creation of weapons for deployment in outer space, and on this basis, under the conditions of mutual trust thus strengthened, immediately begin preparing agreements to reduce the accumulated weapons stocks. To prove its sincerity and goodwill even more convincingly, the Soviet Union has declared that it is unilaterally halting further deployment of its medium-range missiles and suspending the implementation of other countermeasures in Europe until November of this year.

It might seem that, if there was a real intention to reach agreement, these proposals and actions by the Soviet Union, which have been evaluated the world over as an important and constructive goodwill gesture, would be grasped. Yet the U.S. administration has displayed absolutely incomprehensible haste, expressing a negative attitude immediately and describing our actions as "propaganda." Under these conditions, how can we not doubt the sincerity of the intention of the United States at the Geneva talks?

The Soviet Union strives sincerely for the attainment of concrete accords in Geneva and wants Soviet-American relations to return to the channel of normal, mutually advantageous cooperation and mutual respect. Mikhail Gorbachev asked the congressmen to convey this to the Congress and administration of the United States.

Speaker O'Neill and the other American congressmen declared themselves in favor of an improvement in relations between the United States and the Soviet Union and for success at the talks in Geneva. They expressed great satisfaction with the meeting, describing it as frank and useful.

10

REPORT TO
THE PLENARY MEETING
OF THE
CENTRAL COMMITTEE
OF THE CPSU

COMRADES, we are on the eve of the fortieth anniversary of the great victory over fascism. Remembering the huge price paid for the victory by the Soviet people and other peoples of the anti-Hitler coalition, recalling again and again the tragedy that befell mankind, the Communist Party and the Soviet Government consider the main task of their foreign policy to be the prevention of such a tragedy ever occurring again, especially the prevention of a nuclear catastrophe.

The Soviet Union and our Party have been and will forever remain faithful to the sacred memory of the immortal feat of the peoples who routed fascism.

The Soviet Union declares once again that it will pursue steadfastly the Leninist policy of peace and peaceful coexistence which is determined by our social system, morals, and world outlook. We are in favor of stable, correct and, if you like, civilized interstate relations based on a genuine respect for international law. But it must be crystal clear that international relations can be channeled toward normal cooperation only if the imperialists abandon their attempts to solve the historical argument between the two social systems by military means.

The united community of socialist states, its economic and defensive right and its unity of action in the international arena are an invincible force in the struggle for mankind's peaceful future. The attainment of military-strategic balance with the states of the aggressive NATO bloc is a historic achievement of the fraternal countries of socialism. This parity must be preserved by all means for the sake of peace, as it reliably checks the aggressive appetites of imperialism.

As before, we will spare no effort in providing the Soviet Armed Forces with everything necessary for the defense of our country and its allies, to ensure that no one will take us by surprise.

Today mankind has an enormous potential for peace, as well as experience and sufficient historical and social outlook to understand where the policy of aggression can lead. This understanding is more and more firmly uniting the peace forces, stepping up the antiwar and antinuclear movements and mobilizing ever-new progressive and democratic forces for the struggle against the threat of war. It is no surprise that Washington's egoistic militarist policy provokes ever-growing criticism and resistance in many countries. Communist and workers' parties, trade unions, and other mass public organizations are making a great contribution to the common struggle for peace.

No nation wants war. In this fact lie enormous reserves and possibilities for the implementation of the policy of peace and progress. Everything must be done to prevent the forces of militerism and aggression from gaining the upper hand in international relations.

We are convinced that a world war can be averted. However, history has shown that the struggle for peace and universal security is no easy matter; it requires continuous efforts.Through the fault of imperialism, the international situation remains tense and dangerous. Humankind faces a choice: either to exacerbate tensions and confrontations or to search constructively for mutually acceptable agreements which would stop the material preparations for a nuclear conflict.

It must be stated in no uncertain terms that the responsibility for the present situation rests primarily with the ruling circles of the United States. They continue to advocate the arms race and sabotage disarmament. The world public is well aware of this posture. New types of weapons of mass destruction are being developed on their initiative. Today we are witnessing attempts to spread the arms race to outer space. Hundreds of U.S. military bases scattered around the globe are also destabilizing the world situation.

The United States claims openly that it has a "right" to interfere everywhere. It ignores and often openly tramples underfoot the interests of other countries and peoples, the traditions of international relations and current treaties and agreements, it constantly creates seats of conflict and military danger, making the situation in different areas of the world tense. Today the United States is threatening the heroic people of Nicaragua with military reprisals in an attempt to deny them their freedom and sovereignty, as was the case in Grenada. Solidarity with the forces of progress and democracy, with these countries and peoples which, in the face of the reactionary onslaught, are upholding their freedom and independence, is a matter of principle to us. In this respect our course remains as clear-cut as always.

We do not have to possess some special political insight to see how in recent years imperialism has stepped up its subversive activities and how it coordinates its actions against the socialist states. This covers all spheres: political, economic, ideological, and military. Documents of the fraternal parties have stressed repeatedly that imperialism is attempting to stage acts of social revenge on the widest front possible, including the socialist community, the countries liberated from colonial oppression, the national-liberation movements, and the working people in the capitalist countries.

The economic expansion of the United States is growing in scope and intensity. The manipulation of interest rates, the plundering activities of the multinational corporations, the political restrictions in trade and boycotts and sanctions of all kinds are creating a climate of tension and mistrust in international economic relations, destabilizing the world economy and trade and undermining their legal base. The exploitation of recently liberated countries is growing while the process of their economic decolonization is being blocked. By concentrating the growing mass of financial and material resources of other countries in its hands, the United States directly or indirectly places them at the service of its giant military program.

Under these conditions, there is a growing interest around the world in the idea of working out and implementing measures to normalize international economic relations and ensure the economic security of states.

The complexity of the international situation and the acute nature of prevailing tensions obligates us to continue to give top priority to matters of foreign policy.

The over-all improvement and enrichment of cooperation, the development of comprehensive contacts with the fraternal socialist countries, the ensuring of their close cooperation in the political, economic, ideological, defense, and other fields, the concern that the national and international interests of the participants in the great community should be combined organically – all these tasks are becoming increasingly important.

The implementation of the decisions of the economic summit conference of the CMEA member countries held last June is now on the agenda for joint work by the fraternal countries. This goal is demanded persistently by both the council's common interests and the requirements of the socioeconomic development of each state, as well as by the specific features of the international situation.

The exchange of views which we had in the middle of March with the leaders of the parties and the states that are members of the Warsaw Treaty enables us to declare confidently that we are unanimous in our conviction that while NATO exists, the Warsaw Treaty Organization must continue to play an important role in defending the position of socialism in Europe and the world, serving as a reliable instrument for the prevention of nuclear war and the strengthening of international security.

The Soviet Union will purposefully and persistently consolidate mutual contacts and develop cooperation with other socialist countries, including the People's Republic of China. Our position on this matter is well known and remains in force.

We favor further expansion of comprehensive cooperation with the countries of Asia, Africa, and Latin America. The CPSU and the Soviet state invariably support the right of all nations to determine, according to their choice, their present socioeconomic system and to build their future without any outside interference. Trying to deny nations this sovereign right is hopeless and is doomed to failure.

We invariably advocate the development of normal, equal relations with capitalist countries. All controversial issues and conflict situations should be resolved through political means – this is our firm conviction.

The Politburo believes that the international documents of the détente period, including the Helsinki Final Act, have lost none of their importance. They exemplify the way international relations can be built if nations are guided by the principles of equality and equal security, by the realities in the world, if they do not seek any advantages, but mutually acceptable decisions and agreements. In connection with the tenth anniversary of the Conference on Security and Cooperation in Europe, it would be useful if, on behalf of the countries which signed the Final Act, the will to overcome dangerous tension and develop peaceful cooperation and constructive foundations in international life were once again to be expressed in Helsinki.

The Soviet Union is advocating fruitful and all-around economic, scientific and technological cooperation built on the principles of mutual benefit and excluding any sort of discrimination; it is prepared to continue to expand and develop trade relations, to develop new forms of economic relations based on the mutual interest of the sides in the joint mastering of research, engineering and technological innovations, the design and construction of enterprises and in the exploitation of raw material resources.

When posing the question in this manner, it is necessary to analyze the state of our foreign economic relations, to take a closer look at them while taking account of the future. There are favorable opportunities in this field despite international tensions. The approach to mutually advantageous economic relations and foreign trade must be extensive, large scale, and projected into the future.

We are in favor of extensive, versatile and mutually beneficial cooperation with the West European countries, with Japan and with other capitalist countries.

It is common knowledge that we are ready to improve relations with the United States, as well, for mutual benefit and without attempts to impinge on the legitimate rights and interests of one another. There is no fatal inevitability of confrontation between the two countries. If we grasp both the favorable and the unfavorable experiences accumulated in the history of Soviet-American relations, the history—both recent and not so recent—then it must be said that the most reasonable thing to do is to seek for the ways that lead to the improvement of relations and to build the bridge of cooperation from both sides.

However, the first stage in the Geneva talks, which has already been completed, gives us every reason to state that Washington is pursuing a policy of not reaching an agreement with the Soviet

Union. This conclusion can be seen if only from the fact that the United States refuses, in general, to discuss the nonproliferation of the arms race to outer space simultaneously with the discussion of limiting and reducing nuclear weapons. Thus, it violates the agreement reached in January on the relationship between the three aspects: averting the arms race in space, the reduction of strategic nuclear arms, and the reduction of medium-range nuclear weapons in Europe.

The question arises: What is the explanation for such a position? The explanation is that certain circles in the United States still want to achieve a dominant position in the world, especially in the military field. We have often drawn the attention of the U.S. side to the fact that these ambitious plans lack any chance of success. The Soviet Union, its friends and allies and, in fact, all other states that adhere to the positions of peace and peaceful cooperation do not recognize the right of any state or group of states to attain supremacy and to impose their will on other countries and nations.

The Soviet Union has never set a similar goal for itself.

We would like to express the hope that the United States' present position will be corrected. This would provide the opportunity for achieving mutually acceptable agreements. The readiness for this exists on our side.

Evidence of this willingness is the Soviet Union's proposal for both sides to introduce, for the entire period in which the talks are held, a moratorium on the development of space weapons and a freeze on strategic nuclear arsenals. Continuing this line, the Soviet Union has declared unilaterally a moratorium on the deployment of medium-range missiles and the buildup of other countermeasures in Europe. The whole world has looked upon this decision as an important and constructive step which would facilitate the success of the talks.

Our recent moratorium is not the only step in this direction. In 1982 the Soviet Union pledged unilaterally not to be the first to use nuclear weapons. In 1983 it declared unilaterally a moratorium on being the first to place antisatellite weapons in outer space. The U.S. government did not reply to either of these initiatives with even a single gesture of good will. On the contrary, Washington tries to put the activities of the Soviet Union, which are aimed at reducing the danger of war and achieving accords, in a false light, to generate mistrust in them. In other words, everything is being done to avoid positive steps in reply.

People cannot but be surprised at the haste with which the U.S. Administration gives its standard and usual No in reply to our proposals. This is clear evidence of the United States' reluctance to work for reasonable results. I will say one thing: the arms race and talks on disarmament are incompatible—this is clear to anyone who does not resort to hypocrisy and does not pursue the goal of deceiving public opinion. The Soviet Union will not support such a course, and those who are now embarking on political games and not serious politics should be aware of this. We would not like a repitition of the sad experience of the preceding talks.

For its part, the Soviet Union will be persistently working in Geneva to reach practical and mutually acceptable agreements which would make it possible not only to put an end to the arms race but to achieve progress in disarmament. Today as never before we need the political will for the sake of peace on Earth, for the sake of a better tomorrow.

*   *   *

These, comrades, are our tasks and the main trends in our domestic and foreign policies. They will of course be discussed in detail at this Plenary Meeting, which is to determine the nature of the pre-Congress work of the entire Party, of each of its organizations.

We must hold the Plenary Meeting in a way which would allow us to sum it up in Lenin's own words:

"We know our tasks today much more clearly, concretely and thoroughly than we did yesterday; we are not afraid of pointing openly to our mistakes in order to rectify them. We shall now devote all the Party's efforts to improving its organization, to enriching the quality and content of its work, to creating closer contact with the masses, and to working out increasingly correct and accurate work-ing-class tactics and strategy."

The Party and the Soviet people expect from us comprehen-sive, well-thought-out and responsible decisions and it can be said in all confidence that they will be supported by the Communists, by all the people. This support will find its expression in their social awareness, their activity and their work.

April 23, 1985

11

TO THE
PARTICIPANTS
OF THE
TORGAU REUNION

I SEND MY cordial greetings to all who have assembled in Torgau to mark a memorable event: the fortieth anniversary of the meeting of Soviet and American troops on the river Elbe.

The years pass, the decades go by, but the names of those who did not spare their lives to dispel the dark clouds of enslavement and tyranny that hung over mankind live bright in the grateful memory of people.

The veterans of the Great Patriotic War, of that epic battle against the forces of fascist aggression and militarism, are held in high esteem by the entire people of our country. We bow our heads before those who perished in that battle. The present generation owes to them its opportunity to live and work in peace.

During these days, on the eve of celebrating the great victory, Soviet people also pay a tribute of respect to the weighty contribution toward the achievement of the common goal made by the peoples and the armed forces of the United States, Great Britain, France, China, and other member states of the anti-Hitler coalition. In bringing about that victory, an important role was played by the military formations and the partisan armies and detachments of Yugoslavia, Poland, Czechoslovakia, Bulgaria, Rumania, Albania, and Hungary, and by the Resistance Movement in France, Italy, Greece, Beligum, the Netherlands, Norway, Denmark, and Luxembourg. A courageous struggle against Hitlerite nazism was waged by German and Austrian patriots.

Our combat alliance born during the war years showed the potential for cooperation that lies in joint struggle for peace and a better future for humanity. Thus, the handshake of the Soviet and American soldiers who met in the spring of 1945 on the Elbe has gone down in history forever as a symbol of hope and friendship.

Today, as well, the duty of all honest men, young and veterans alike, is to do all they can to prevent the fire of war from scarring our earth.

In recalling events of the past war, we ponder the present and, of course, think of the future: of a just and stable peace, of saving the peoples of the world from the nuclear threat.

Not hostility and discord, but mutual understanding and cooperation among countries and peoples should serve as the beacon for mankind. The Soviet people are convinced that constructive cooperation among the former Allies, among all states, in the struggle to safeguard peace can and should become a powerful factor in improving the international climate.

Those who today again link hands over the Elbe show a good example of that.

From the bottom of my heart I wish the heroic veterans, those who fought against Hitlerite fascism, their families and all the participants in the meeting in Torgau the best of health and many years of a happy and peaceful life.

Mikhail Gorbachev
April 26, 1985

12

SPEECH AT THE RECEPTION IN WARSAW

PERMIT ME, on behalf of the Soviet delegation and of all participants in the meeting, first and foremost to express cordial gratitude for hospitality to the leaders of the Polish United Workers' Party and the Polish state. We also convey fraternal greetings to the inhabitants of the heroic and beautiful city of Warsaw, to all the working people of Poland, and wishes of success in the building of socialism.

An act of historic importance has taken place here today, in Warsaw, the city which gave its name to our alliance. The Treaty on Friendship, Cooperation and Mutual Assistance, concluded thirty years ago, has been prolonged. Prolonged, as comrade Jaruzelski said, with the conviction that our alliance is vitally necessary to all its participants, necessary for the strengthening of peace and the security of the peoples.

Vladimir Ilyich Lenin emphasized that a revolution must be able to defend itself. And, in the Warsaw Treaty, the peoples of our countries have found a true defender of the revolutionary gains. What has the Warsaw Treaty given to all of us? It has given us the possibility of peaceful, constructive labor. The inviolability of frontiers has been secured reliably. A firm barrier has been put up in the way of the latter-day enemies of socialism and claimants to world supremacy.

History has not known another such alliance as ours where relations are founded on full equality and comradely mutual assistance of sovereign states; an alliance which is an alliance of the peoples in the true sense of the term; an alliance which does not threaten anyone, but is dedicated wholly to the defense of peace. We build our relations with countries of the other social system on the principle of peaceful coexistence—the only reasonable basis, especially in the nuclear age.

The major initiatives put forward by our countries and aimed at strengthening peace in Europe and detente are linked with the Warsaw Treaty. Today's meeting reaffirmed the common readiness to continue collectively to seek ways to eliminate the threat of war and expanding international cooperation. We are in favor of easing confrontation between the two military-political alliances, which would be in the interest of all the peoples of the world.

It is not the Soviet Union and other socialist states that laid the basis for the division of Eruope and the postwar world. This was done by the architects of NATO, while our alliance came into existence only six years later. Since then, on more than one occasion, we have expressed our readiness to disband the Warsaw Treaty Organization if NATO agrees to reciprocate. This principled position has been preserved fully. But, regrettably, the other side did not have and still does not have any such intention. On the contrary, new aggressive doctrines are being advanced in NATO before our very eyes, with both nuclear and conventional arms being built up at an accelerated pace. And this compels us to think now of further strengthening the Warsaw Treaty Organization.

Humanity is faced with an alternative: either it will correct the unfavorable course of events, or the danger of nuclear war will grow. And this danger is being intensified many times over by US military plans in outer space. No matter what their initiators may say to justify them, the essence of these plans is clear: to have an opportunity to deliver the first nuclear strike and to deliver it with impunity. Since the United States and NATO categorically refuse to follow the example of the Soviet Union and assume an obligation not to be the first to use nuclear weapons, their intentions acquire an even more dangerous character.

The development of "Star Wars" weapons is just beginning. But this increases tension in the modern world and leads to the distabilization of the entire system of international relations, to even sharper political and military confrontation than now. This should not be forgotten by both the initiaters of the above mentioned provocative scheme and those who are inclined to take part in it.

We have a fundamentally different approach: not to turn space into a new source of military danger, not to develop space attack weapons, and to destroy the existing antisatelite systems. Simultaneously, we propose that agreement be reached on a radical reduction of nuclear weapons and, in general, work be carried out for the complete elimination of nuclear arms.

Such a simple and natural step as freezing the nuclear potential of both sides suggests itself. We are told that to accept this means to consolidate Soviet military superiority. But, first, there is no such superiority. We have proved this repeatedly with figures, and Washington has never been able to refute them. And, second, who said that we want to stop at the freeze? On the contrary, we insist that a freeze should be followed by a cardinal reduction of nuclear arms.

We have already suggested that both sides should begin by reducing strategic offensive arms by one-quarter. But we would have no objections to carrying out greater reductions. All this is possible if the arms race does not begin in space, if space remains peaceful.

The Soviet Union and other Warsaw Treaty countries do not seek superiority either on earth or in outer space. We do not aim to compete in who will build a higher nuclear fence. But neither will we allow the military-strategic parity to be upset. This is the common firm stand of the parties to the Warsaw Treaty. If preparations for "Star Wars" continue, we shall have no choice but to take countermeasures, including, of course, the strengthening and improvement of offensive nuclear arms.

The first round of the Soviet-American talks on nuclear and space weapons, which has just ended, has shown that they are proceeding with great difficulty. It is clear that the talks can be successful only if the principle of equality and equal security, and the agreement on the ultimate aim of the talks and on the interrelated solution of the questions under discussion are observed.

As has been announced already, the Soviet Union has unilaterally suspended the deployment of medium-range missiles and the implementation of other countermeasures in Europe. The moratorium went into effect on April 7. This step of ours has been appraised correctly by the world public, and also by many sober-minded U.S. and West European politicians. We have a right to expect that Washington and the capitals of other NATO countries will approach the assessment of our initiative more seriously and thoughtfull and will display restraint on the issue of deploying American missiles in Western Europe. After all, reciprocity in this area would help move the Geneva talks onto the plane of practical solutions and would also play a role in solving more complex problems.

The Warsaw Treaty has been in force for almost a third of a century, and in all this time it has been the initiator of constructive ideas aimed at easing tension and arms limitation, at promoting all European cooperation. Its growing importance in international politics has had a positive influence on the overall world climate. And this is a result of collective efforts, of the contribution of each of the fraternal countries.

Comrades, on the eve of the fortieth anniversary of the great victory over fascism, we again recall the oath of the victors before the graves and ruins of World War II: there must be no more war! We remember this; we remember the lessons of the war. And one of the greatest lessons consists in the example of cooperation between the countries of the anti-Hitler coalition. Today we call upon all the states of Europe and other continents to rise above the differences and become partners in the struggle against a new danger threatening the whole of humankind: the danger of nuclear destruction.

In prolonging the Warsaw Treaty, we again express our firm conviction that war can and must be averted by joint effort. Such is the will of the peoples of our countries. The policy of our Parties and governments, and the entire activity of the defensive alliance of the socialist states are directed toward this.

To the further cooperation of our parties and states, to the consolidation of their unity and cohesion on the principles of Marxism-Leninism and socialist internationalism!

May the fraternal alliance of the socialist countries — the Warsaw Treaty Organization — grow strong!

To people's socialist Poland, to the health of Comrade Jaruzelski and members of the Polish leadership, and all participants in our meeting!

To a lasting peace on earth!

April 25, 1985

13

LETTER TO THE FRENCH ASSOCIATION OF WAR VETERANS

IT WAS with great attentiveness that I read your message, permeated as it is with interest in the success of the current Soviet-US negotiations in Geneva, where questions of paramount importance for the destiny of peace, for the entire human race are being discussed.

War veterans know better than anybody else just what war means and work persistently to prevent any further outbreak, and especially of a war involving nuclear weapons capable of reducing our planet to ashes.

I can assure you: the Soviet Union went to Geneva with the firm intention of holding constructive talks aimed at preventing the militarization of outer space and radically reducing strategic nuclear weapons and medium-range weapons. Since it would be pointless to hold negotiations on the reduction of arms while at the same time building them up, we proposed that the Soviet Union and the USA should introduce, for the duration of the talks, a moratorium on the development (including research), testing and deployment of strike space weapons and should freeze their strategic offensive arms. At the same time, the deployment of U.S. medium-range missiles in Europe should be terminated and, likewise, the Soviet Union's countermeasures.

To facilitate the search for agreement we, as you know, introduced a unilateral moratorium, starting on April 7 of this year, on the deployment of our medium-range missiles, and suspended other countermeasures in Europe taken in response to the siting of the new U.S. missiles. That is, we confirmed our desire to reach agreement with concrete actions which have met with a positive response in the world.

This is our unswerving and principled policy. The USSR is sincerely striving for disarmament and nuclear arms reduction. Back in 1982 our country pledged not to be the first to use nuclear weapons and urged other nuclear powers to follow suit. In 1983 the USSR declared a unilateral moratorium on the deployment of anti-satellite weapons in space for as long as other states did likewise.

Both these pledges remain in effect to this day. We also proposed that the USSR and the USA should reduce their strategic offensive arms by one quarter or more. But the US administration has given no constructive reply to any of these initiatives.

Unfortunately, even now, judging by the first stage of the Geneva negotiations, the U.S. representatives display no desire to reach agreement. Something else is clear: The USA is carrying on a reckless arms race and is actively trying to project it into space.

Success in Geneva is dependent on the political good will of both sides to come to agreement, with strict observance of the principle of equality and equal security. Despite the complicated and tense situation in the world and difficulties in the Geneva negotiations we remain realistically optimisitc.

We hope our partners will heed the voice of the peoples who want peace and an end to the arms race. We hope that common sense, political realism and a feeling of responsibility for a peaceful future will prevail. We have faith in the ability of nations to safeguard their right to life.

Soviet people are now widely marking the 40th anniversary of the great Victory. They give due credit to the contribution of their anti-Hitler coalition Allies to the total defeat of hated fascism. We remember the courageous French patriots — soldiers and Resistance fighters who made a notable contribution to our common victory.

It is our firm conviction that no task is more important in the world today than to avert the threat of nuclear annihilation. The more actively and resolutely members of the public work toward fulfilling this task, the better are the chances of success.

                                        Mikhail Gorbachev
                                        May 7, 1985

14

INTERVIEW WITH THE PRESS TRUST OF INDIA

QUESTION: On the eve of your meeting with our Prime Minister, what could you say about the state and prospects of Soviet-Indian relations in the context of the struggle for peace and disarmament?

Answer: First of all, I would like to stress that Indian leaders are received with a special feeling here, reflecting the sincere sympathy and respect of the Soviet people for the great and friendly people of India. Different generations of Soviet and Indian people have written shining chapters into the history of our friendship, whose development was so much promoted by Jawaharlal Nehru and Indira Gandhi.

Our attitude toward India reflects the Soviet Union's principled and invariable support for the struggle of nations against imperialist oppression, for stronger independence and social renewal. This course was bequeathed to us by the great Lenin, and we are undeviatingly committed to it. We have inherited what can be called without exaggeration a unique, priceless asset.

Indira Gandhi said that we were bound not only by relations between the governments or even by political and economic cooperation alone, but that our relations were the intertwining of the ardent hearts of our two creator-nations. Her vivid words describe the level and the entire multiformity of our relations aptly.

I would like to take this opportunity to pay tribute once again to the bright memory of the outstanding daughter of the Indian people, whose name is forever inscribed in the history of the Indian people, whose name is forever inscribed in the history of *Soviet-Indian friendship.* The International Lenin Prize "For the Promotion of Peace Among Nations" awarded to her is a recognition of her tremendous contribution to the struggle for durable peace and friendship among nations.

An Indian saying has it that a road on which people meet each other halfway is the shortest. Our two peoples have been following exactly such a road for decades. This is precisely why our relations have been on the rise. The high level, dynamism, and comprehen-

sive nature of our relations, based on the Treaty of Peace, Friendship and Cooperation, is a source of satisfaction to us.

We greatly appreciate India's contribution to the collective
effort to preserve peace and remove the nuclear threat. Heading the
nonaligned movement, which has become a major factor in international relations, India is doing much to strengthen its unity and
beneficial influence in the world.

Soviet-Indian friendship is an asset not just of our two peoples
alone. It is an important factor for peace and stability in the current
tense situation and an example of how fruitfully countries with
different systems can cooperate if they are guided by the ideals of
peace, by the principles of mutual respect and of equitable cooperation.

We are optimistic about the prospects of Soviet-Indian relations. The last time Prime Minister Rajiv Gandhi and I met, we
reaffirmed our desire to strengthen our cooperation further. I'm sure
that the forthcoming discussion of a broad range of issues on
bilateral and international relations will give a new content to our
traditional ties in the interests of the Soviet and Indian peoples and
of peace in Asia and worldwide.

And, naturally, I personally will be pleased to resume talks with
the Indian leader, who is respected greatly in our country.

Question: The initiatives of the heads of state and government
of six countries representing four continents, embodied in their
declarations of 1984 and 1985, have generally been welcomed in the
Soviet Union. How do you think they could be put into practice?

Answer: We have a high opinion of those initiatives. The ideas
voiced in the documents of the heads of six countries and the Soviet
initiatives go in the same direction. The ultimate goal put forward in
the declarations—to eliminate nuclear weapons from mankind's
life—corresponds fully to the goals of our country's foreign policy.

Entering into the Geneva talks with the United States, we
agreed that their aim was to prevent an arms race in space, to
terminate it on earth and to begin radical reductions of nuclear arms
leading to their complete elimination.

It is possible to begin with what the leaders of the six proposed:
to stop the development, production, and deployment of nuclear

weapons, to freeze nuclear arsenals and embark on their reduction, to prevent the arms race from spreading to space, and to conclude a treaty banning all nuclear tests.

We have proposed stopping further arms buildup as a first step, and that the Soviet Union and the United States should impose a moratorium on the development—including research—testing, and deployment of strike space weapons for the duration of the Geneva negotiations and freeze their strategic offensive armaments, and that the deployment of U.S. medium-range missiles in Europe and the buildup of our countermeasures be discontinued.

The Soviet Union has already unilaterally imposed a moratorium until this November on the deployment of its medium-range missiles and suspended the implementation of other countermeasures in Europe. True to its word, the Soviet Union abides strictly by the terms of this moratorium. We are entitled to hope for a more serious and thoughtful assessment of our initiative by Washington and its NATO partners, and for restraint in regard to the deployment of U.S. missiles in Western Europe. Reciprocity in this matter could help place the Geneva talks on a practical footing.

And, finally, about stopping nuclear weapons tests. We have repeatedly urged the United States and other nuclear powers to do so. The Soviet Union has proposed that the states that possess nuclear weapons announce a moratorium on any nuclear explosions to be in effect until the conclusion of a treaty on the complete general prohibition of nuclear weapons tests. It could be instituted as of August 6, 1985—i.e., on the fortieth anniversary of the tragic atomic bombing of Hiroshima, or even earlier.

The Soviet Union is also ready to resume immediately the talks on the complete prohibition of nuclear weapons tests, which were broken off through the fault of the United States. It is high time to put into effect the Soviet-American treaties on the Limitation of Underground Nuclear Weapons Tests and on Underground Nuclear Explosions for Peaceful Purposes, which were signed in 1974 and 1976, respectively. They have not yet been ratified—again not through the fault of the Soviet side.

Of course, special responsibility for the destiny of the world rests today with the nuclear powers, and primarily with the Soviet

Union and the United States. But the Soviet Union has never looked at the world in the context of Soviet-American relations alone. We are deeply convinced that all states can and must be involved in a search for realistic solutions to urgent problems and in efforts to ease international tensions. The voice of millions of people in different countries in favor of effective measures to end the arms race and reduce arms stockpiles, against attempts to use negotiations as a cover for the continuation of this race, is of tremendous importance.

Question: What could you say about the prospects of attaining durable peace and developing cooperation in Asia, specifically, in the Indian Ocean area?

Answer: I would like to stress that we value highly India's contribution to the strengthening of peace and stability in Asia, its realistic and considered approach to the key issues of the region.

The Soviet Union has always advocated peace and security in Asia, as well as equitable cooperation between Asian states. This applies fully to the Indian Ocean area. We support the idea of proclaiming it a zone of peace.

It is common knowledge that for several years now the United States has been impeding the convening of an international conference on this issue. It has also unilaterally broken off the Soviet-American talks on limiting military activity in the Indian Ocean. In the meantime, the United States is constantly building up its military presence there.

The Soviet Union repeatedly has voiced its readiness to resume the talks. At the Soviet-Indian summit in 1982, the Soviet Union proposed that all states whose ships use the waters of the Indian Ocean refrain from any steps which might aggravate the situation in the region, even before the convening of the conference. This Soviet proposal is still in effect. Specifically, the states in question should not send large naval formations there and should not hold military exercises, and those nonlittoral countries which have military bases in the region should not expand or modernize them.

Recently the drive for a zone of peace in the Indian Ocean has focused on the question of convening an international conference on the issue. I would like to stress our desire to work vigorously with other interested states to make such a forum possible, so that the Indian Ocean could ultimately become a sphere of vital interests of the states situated on its shores, and not others; a zone of peace rather than of tensions and conflicts.

In conclusion, let me, through your agency, wish happiness, prosperity and peace to the Indian people. We wish the government and all the citizens of India success in the efforts to further consolidate national unity and cohesion, in the work for the social progress and prosperity of your great country.

*   *   *

During the talk following the handing to the correspondent of the replies to the questions of the PTI Agency, Mikhail Gorbachev emphasized that the Soviet Union attaches great importance to the forthcoming visit of Prime Minister Rajiv Gandhi and believes that this visit will be a significant event in the lives of the two states and in the development of mutual relations. Such has always been the case: Each visit by leaders of our countries and each of their meetings has left a noticeable mark on Soviet-Indian relations. In this context, we in the Soviet Union recall with warmth and great respect the visits to our country of the outstanding leaders of India, Jawaharlal Nehru and Indira Gandhi.

We are confident that Prime Minister Rajiv Gandhi's visit will also do a lot to develop further Soviet-Indian cooperation and to contribute to our joint struggle for lasting peace and stronger international security. There are good personal contacts between us, and we hope to augment them still further.

Friendship with India and deep respect for its great people, their rich ancient culture and their contribution to human progress — all this, I can say, is in the hearts of all Soviet citizens.

Friendship with India has also been an active tradition of our foreign policy for decades. A united, strong, peace-loving India is an integral and very necessary part of the modern world.

Personally, I take an enormous interest in your country, and I hope that Prime Minister Rajiv Gandhi's kind invitation will enable

me, at an appropriate time, to have a close look at India and its
people.

*   *   *

Mikhail Gorbachev replied to a few additional questions put by
the correspondent.

In response to the question about which factors he ascribes the
successful development of his activity as Party leader, Mikhail
Gorbachev pointed out that the "secret" here is simply the Soviet
socialist way of life, the conditions which the socialist system
creates for the formation and development of the individual. The
labor training received in a family of farm workers, like the one
millions of children of workers, farmers and intellectuals get in our
country; a good education, access to which everybody enjoys in our
country; and the social and political school I have passed through,
first in the Komsomol and then the Party—all these are typical
factors for our way of life, that enable Soviet citizens in one sector
or another to participate actively in the development of the country
and in the construction of the new life. Able persons can be found in
each country, in each people, but, we believe, it is the socialist
system that creates the best conditions for their development and for
the socially useful application of their abilities.

Some politicians in the West, said S. P. K. Gupta, noting the
energy and dynamic way in which the Soviet Union is pursuing its
policy, express apprehension that the materialization of its plans in
the field of foreign policy and the implementation of its planned
measures in the fields of social and economic development might
pose a growing threat to the West and, notably, to the United States.
The correspondent asked Mikhail Gorbachev's opinion.

Mikhail Gorbachev said that this kind of "apprehensions"
should be left to the conscience of those Western leaders and
officials who are voicing them. The leadership of our Party and
state have been making formidable efforts recently to ensure an
acceleration in the peaceful socioeconomic development of the
country. We have tried to make a realistic appraisal of the situation
in various fields of economic life, have consulted with experts and
have discussed these issues with a wide range of urban and rural
workers. As a result, we have an outline of a program whose

accomplishment will secure the achievement of the goals which the Party and the people are undertaking. We hope to complete work on the main directions of the strategy for our socioeconomic development by the time of the 27th CPSU Congress, in 1986, and are certain that our plans will be approved by the Party and by all Soviet people.

Since the Soviet Union is undertaking major and far-reaching tasks of peaceful development, naturally we need durable peace and will do everything within our power to preserve and consolidate peace on our planet. We are positive that here our interests coincide with the interests of all the peoples in the socialist, advanced capitalist, and newly free Asian, African and Latin American countries. This desire for peace probably does not suit some groups of imperialists who would like to preserve international tensions and to continue the arms race, using it for their narrow selfish goals, but this is a totally different matter. As for ourselves, we believe that our policy meets the interests of both the Soviet people and the peoples of other countries.

May 9, 1985

15

THE
IMMORTAL EXPLOITS
OF THE
SOVIET PEOPLE

COMRADES, returning now in our minds and hearts to the victorious spring of 1945, we ask naturally whether the hopes of the millions of people who fought so that we, our children and grandchildren could live in peace and happiness have materialized.

Yes, they have! But a great deal remains to be done to preserve our planet, the common home of mankind, both for us, who are living now, and for future generations, and to eliminate wars from people's lives once and for all.

Forty years is not a short period of time by any standards. Time passes. Those who were born after the victory have become mature people, and their children are grown up, too. For most people today, the Second World War is an event outside their personal experience. But the war left such a legacy that its results and lessons continue to influence the whole course and nature of the world's development and the people's consciousness.

World War II emerged long before the first battles took place on the fields of Europe and on the ocean expanses. Its sinister shadow was looming over humankind when some politicians failed and others did not want to prevent nazism from coming to power. Today we have better knowledge than we did at that time about who helped and how they helped the nazi ruling clique to arm itself, to build up a potential for aggression and prepare for military adventures.

The attempts by leading groups of monopoly capital to manipulate German fascism's expansion, directing it eastward, were the height of political irresponsibility. The Munich Pact will go down forever in the book of shame covering the names of those who so persistently instigated Hitler to attack the Soviet Union. One has to suffer from profound political amnesia not to remember this.

There is no need now to recall the names of the bourgeois politicians and statesmen of the 1930s who erred sincerely and those who were motivated by their selfish class interests. History will not change its verdict: the "Munich policy" of the Western powers and their connivance at nazi aggression resulted in a great tragedy for all the peoples of Europe. The policy pursued by those who, ignoring persistent calls from the Soviet Union, refused to act in a united front to stop the nazi adventurists was criminal. Time will never lift from them the responsibility for a holocaust which could have been prevented if hostility toward socialism had not blinded the leaders of the West at that time.

Unfortunately, history is repeating itself. And today, more than ever before, it is imperative to display vigilance against the intrigues of those who are pushing the world to an abyss, only this time a nuclear abyss. We should have a clear idea from where the threat to humankind is emanating today. The Soviet Union makes this statement just as forcefully as before the war, warning against the menacing danger. Another reason for emphasizing this point is that the ill-intentioned myth of a "Soviet military threat," exploited so noisily by nazism, is still in circulation.

Despite all the efforts of the falsifiers of history to rewrite it, the peoples of the world know that the Soviet Union was the first country to sound the alarm and warn against the growing danger of fascism. It was the Communists who proposed a clear-cut program of struggle against the "brown plague" when it was still in its infancy. Last but not least, it was the Soviet Union that put forward a series of proposals aimed at curbing the aggressor who was casting off all restraint. But at that time, too, it was all dismissed as "communist propaganda."

The occupation of almost the whole of Western Europe, the seizure of Paris, the bombardment of London and the attack on Pearl Harbor dashed those cynical calculations and illusory hopes. It was only after the Soviet Army had won a number of brilliant victories that agreements on cooperation with the Soviet Union in the struggle against fascism began to materialize.

The expansion of the fascist threat made Western politicians look at the world in a more realistic fashion. The history of the anti-Hitler coalition shows indisputably that states with different social systems can join forces in the fight against a common enemy, find mutually acceptable solutions, and work effectively for a common cause.

Soviet people remember the material help which the Allies

gave this country. Though it was not as great as the West is wont to claim, we are nevertheless grateful for that help and regard it as a symbol of cooperation. Though belated, the opening of the Second Front in Europe was a substantial contribution to the common struggle.

The favorable atmosphere of cooperation between the countries of the anti-Hitler coalition and a realistic assessment of the new situation in the world after the defeat of fascism were reflected in the postwar settlement and in the decisions made by the Allied conferences in Teheran, Yalta, and Potsdam. Those decisions, along with the United Nations Charter and other international agreements of that time are imbued with a spirit of cooperation. They ensured that a solution would be found to the complex problems of the postwar settlement, including territorial questions, a settlement meeting the objective of attaining the long-awaited peace.

It is particularly appropriate to recall all these things today when all peoples have one common enemy, the threat of nuclear war, and one supreme goal, removing this threat.

Twice in this century the imperialist forces unleashed bloody world wars in a bid to achieve their class aims, strengthen their positions, and further their selfish interests. But history decreed otherwise. No wonder that both wars, which started out as ventures of imperialism — arrogant, confident of its impunity and convinced that international law was written with the invader's fist — ended in the defeat of those who unleashed them and provoked each time a series of crises which shook the very system that breeds war.

In defending their country's freedom and independence, the Soviet people also carried out the great internationalist mission of saving world civilization from fascism. The defeat of fascism consolidated the positions of progressive democratic forces, which resulted in the triumph of a new social system in a number of European and Asian countries. The first workers' and peasants' state was also born on German soil. During the popular struggle against nazism and Japanese imperialism, a struggle which closely merged with the aspirations of the masses for deep social change, the appeal of socialist ideas grew visibly, while the Communist parties in many countries gained in strength and developed into powerful forces.

The postwar years have seen the formation of a world socialist system and its considerable progress; a community of socialist states has emerged. The new social system that has established itself in the world has proved its vitality. It has awakened the creative power of millions and enabled historic accomplishments to be achieved within a short period of time. Today socialism is a mighty world system, one that is exerting enormous influence on the development of humankind and its future, and is an invincible factor for peace and a guarantor of the security of the peoples.

The states of this great community possess invaluable experience and an efficient mechanism for coordinating their policy. They act as one on international matters and steadfastly uphold the cause of peace and disarmament and the principles of peaceful coexistence. The Warsaw Treaty Organization, its Political Consultative Committee, and the joint armed forces of the allied countries have a special role to play in this respect. So long as there is a threat to peace and security, the Warsaw Treaty members will do everything necessary, as they have always done to safeguard themselves against any encroachments. Proof of this has been provided by the extension of the treaty for another term unanimously approved by all its signatories.

Profound changes in the postwar world have also taken place following the collapse of colonialism, with dozens of independent states springing up where colonies and semicolonies used to be. True, their development has been uneven; there have been ups and downs, achievements and tragedies. True, the developing countries are faced with very difficult problems: some inherited from the past and some due to the policy of neocolonialism.

But it is also true that the system of colonialism has now been eradicated almost completely and that many young national states are playing an increasingly prominent and progressive role in world politics. With the active support of the socialist countries, they are making persistent efforts to establish a new and fairer world economic order. The nonaligned movement has become an important factor in today's international relations.

As we see, comrades, the political map of the world has undergone radical changes in the forty years that have passed since the victory.

The sphere in which imperialism is able to dominate has narrowed perceptibly. Its opportunities for maneuvering and for imposing its will with impunity on sovereign states and peoples have been reduced substantially. The alignment of forces inside the capitalist world has also changed. The defeat in the Second World War of such a predator as German imperialism, the defeat of militarist Japan, and the weakening of the once-powerful British and French rivals of U.S. imperialism have enabled it to lead the capitalist world in all the major indicators: economic, financial and military. The fact that the United States is actually the only major country to have enriched itself fabulously from the war has also boosted the claims of the U.S. ruling class to world hegemony.

In the very first years of the postwar period, imperialist reaction, displeased with the social and international political results of the war, tried to take a kind of historical revenge, to roll back socialism and other democratic forces. This strategy was spearheaded against the Soviet Union while the economic might of the United States and its temporary monopoly of atomic weapons served as levers. This monopoly was looked upon by the ruling circles in the United States as a means of pressuring us and other socialist countries militarily and politically, and for intimidating all people.

That is why, when we speak about the results of the decades since the war, it would be wrong to see only those which we welcome and support sincerely. Unfortunately, we see many things that cause growing anxiety. Of course, the world today does not in the least resemble the world of the 1930s, but by no means has everyone in the West given up attempts to use threats when talking to the Soviet Union.

The cold war launched by militaristic circles in the West was nothing more than an attempt to revise the results of World War II, to deprive the Soviet people, the world forces of progress and democracy of the fruits of their victory. Actually, these goals were never concealed. They found their expression in the ideology and policy of "rolling back socialism," "massive retaliation," "brinksmanship," and so forth. This attitude undermined trust between nations and greatly reduced the opportunities for the constructive international cooperation which has been launched within the framework of the anti-Hitler coalition.

U.S. militarism is in the forefront of the forces that threaten mankind with war. In international relations, the United State's increasingly bellicose policies have become a constant negative factor, which we cannot afford to overlook. The aggressive designs of the U.S. ruling elite have revealed itself in its attempts to upset the military-strategic balance, the bulwark of international security, in its instigation of the arms race, especially the nuclear arms race, and in its dangerous plans for the militarization of space. Some barbarous doctrines and concepts concerning the use of nuclear weapons are being devised, and hundreds of military bases and facilities have been set up around the world. A policy of state-backed terrorism is being pursued in Nicaragua, and an undeclared war is being waged against Afghanistan.

The United States has been trying to impose on the world community of nations its claims for an exclusive and special mission in history. Nothing else can explain its imperial demands for "zones of vital interests," for the "right" to interfere in the internal affairs of other states, to "encourage" or "punish" sovereign nations in any way that suits Washington. Even the United States' political and legal commitments are being violated.

It should be said in quite definite terms that the danger of West German revanchism, in whose revival the current U.S. leadership is so deeply involved, has been growing. The leaders of the seven leading capitalist states, who gathered in Bonn the other day to "mark" the fortieth anniversary of the end of the Second World War in their own way, even dared to question the territorial and political realities in Europe that had emerged as a result of nazi Germany's defeat and postwar developments. Some politicians are to be found who are prepared to forget and even justify the SS cutthroats — moreover, to render homage to them — which is an insult to the very memory of the millions shot, burned, and gassed.

Realizing the scope of the military danger and being aware of our responsibility for the future of the world, we will not let the military and strategic balance between the Soviet Union and the

United States, between the Warsaw Treaty Organization and NATO, be upset. We will continue to pursue this policy because we have learned well, once and for all, what history has taught us.

To put it briefly, the situation remains complicated and even dangerous, but we believe there are genuine opportunities for curbing the forces of militarism. The conviction that a world without wars and weapons can really be reached, that such a world can be built in our own time, that now, today, we should actively strive for it, struggle for it, is becoming implanted strongly in the minds of people the world over.

This conviction is being proved by the experience of the policy of peaceful coexistence and the practical results of cooperation between the states of the two systems. There are many examples. They are encouraging more and more people to oppose aggression and violence in international relations. There is growing realization that peace will be durable if peaceful and constructive coexistence, equal and mutually beneficial cooperation between states with different social systems become supreme universal laws governing international relations. There can be no doubt that the antiwar movement will continue to grow, more and more effectively obstructing adventurist moves by the forces of aggression.

The only sensible way out today is to promote vigorous cooperation between all states in the interests of a universal peaceful future, and also establish, utilize and develop those international mechanisms and institutions that would enable us to balance the interests of individual peoples and countries with the interests of mankind as a whole.

We urge the most diverse social and political forces to promote sincere cooperation based on goodwill for the sake of peace. It is a far from easy task which cannot be solved on a short-term basis and requires a sufficiently high degree of trust in relations between nations. The course of events could be altered radically if tangible progress were attained at the Soviet-American talks on nuclear and space weapons in Geneva. This is our conviction.

The experience of the 1970s is highly invaluable in this respect. At that time good political, legal, moral, and psychological foundations were laid for the cooperation between the states belonging to the two systems in new historical circumstances, covering, for example, such sensitive areas as the security of sides. But the results could have been even more substantial had the West shown a responsible attitude toward the gains of détente.

We are solidly in favor of the process of détente being restarted. But that does not mean simply going back to what was achieved in the 1970s. We must set our sights much higher. Détente is not the ultimate objective of politics. It is an indispensable—yet no more than transitional—stage from a world crammed with weapons to a reliable and comprehensive system of international security.

The Soviet Union is prepared to proceed along these lines. Looking for every opportunity to remove the danger of nuclear war must become the highest duty of governments and responsible statesmen.

I would like to repeat once more today, on this anniversary which is memorable for all of us, that the Soviet Union is resolutely in favor of a world without wars, a world without arms. We declare again and again that the outcome of historical competition between the two systems cannot be decided by military means.

Our allegiance to the policy of peaceful coexistence is evidence of the strength of the new social system and of our faith in its historic potential. This allegiance meets the interests of all nations and peoples. It is permeated with a spirit of true humanism, with the ideals of peace and freedom that also inspired the Soviet people in the years of the last war.

To uphold man's sacred right to live, to ensure a lasting peace, is the duty of the living to the millions of those who fell defending freedom and social progress, our common duty to present and future generations.

May 8, 1985

16

MEETING
WITH
MALCOLM BALDRIDGE

O<small>N</small> MAY 20, 1985 Mikhail Gorbachev, General Secretary of the CPSU Central Committee, received U.S. Secretary of Commerce Malcolm Baldridge in the Kremlin. Baldridge arrived in Moscow as head of a U.S. delegation to a session of the intergovernmental Soviet-American Commercial Commission, and had a conversation with him. Taking part in the conversation were Nikolai Patolichev, Minister of Foreign Trade of the Soviet Union and head of the Soviet delegation to the commission's session, Arthur Hartman, U.S. Ambassador to the Soviet Union, and Jack Matlock, a White House official.

Malcolm Baldridge handed Mikhail Gorbachev a letter from U.S. President Ronald Reagan expressing in general terms a wish for expanding trade between the United States and the Soviet Union.

Mikhail Gorbachev said that the unsatisfactory state of Soviet-American trade and economic ties at the present time was a result of the U.S. administration's policy of discrimination against the Soviet Union, attempts to interfere in the Soviet Union's internal affairs and to use trade as a means of political pressure.

*   *   *

In general, such a state of affairs in the trade and economic sphere, Mikhail Gorbachev emphasized, is a result of the complex and tense political relations that have developed between the two countries in recent years. The Soviet Union did not want such a state of relations and did not contribute toward it. We stand for stable relations with the United States based on equality and respect for each other's legitimate interests. The policy of confrontation, which was a failure in the not-too-distant past, is especially dangerous today because it is *fraught with the threat* of disastrous consequences for many peoples, including the American people. Meanwhile, experience shows that there are objective prerequisites for effective and mutually advantageous cooperation between the

Soviet Union and the United States in different fields. Obviously, it is high time to unfreeze the potential of Soviet-American cooperation, and to freeze — or, to be more precise — to curb the arms race and the escalation of hostility. In this respect, business ties between both countries can play a role. There exist possibilities for that, but only on the basis of equality and mutual benefit, without any discrimination whatsoever. The main goal is to restore the climate of mutual trust in relations between our countries.

*   *   *

Some other aspects of Soviet-American relations were also discussed.

17

SPEECH
AT A DINNER
IN THE KREMLIN
IN HONOR OF
INDIAN PRIME MINISTER
RAJIV GANDHI

Page 1

Mikhail Gorbachev visiting the Khatyn Memorial near Minsk erected in honor of the Byelorussians killed during Second World War.

Page 2, top photo

At the invitation of the USSR Supreme Soviet, Speaker Thomas J. O'Neill, U.S. House of Representatives, visits Mikhail Gorbachev.

Page 2, bottom photo

British Prime Minister Margaret Thatcher visits Mikhail Gorbachev in the Kremlin on March 13, 1985. They had met earlier in Great Britain.

Page 3, top photo

Mikhail Gorbachev and Andrei Gromyko at a meeting with the new Prime Minister of Canada, Brian Mulroney.

Page 3, bottom photo:

At the Kirov Tractor Factory in Leningrad. May 15, 1985.

Page 4, top photo

Mikhail Gorbachev and Andrei Gromyko with Vice President George Bush and U.S. Secretary of State George Shultz in the Kremlin.

Page 4, bottom photo

A group of U.S. Senators meet with Mikhail Gorbachev in the Kremlin: Strom Thurmond, Sam Nunn and Robert C. Byrd. September 3, 1985.

Page 5

On his tour of the USSR, Mikhail Gorbachev gets together with residents of Urengoi, a rapidly growing city in Western Siberia. September 5, 1985.

Page 6, top photo

Mikhail Gorbachev talks with instructors at the Leningrad Polytechnical Institute, a leading educational establishment in the Soviet Union.

Page 6, bottom photo

Mikhail Gorbachev and his wife, Raisa, on a visit to Tselinograd in Kazakhstan (Central Asia), second largest republic in the Soviet Union.

Page 7

Mikhail Gorbachev addressing students at School No. 514 in Moscow. April 17, 1985.

Page 8

From the Gorbachevs' personal album: The top photo is a family portrait, the bottom photo shows Mikhail Gorbachev and his wife Raisa on vacation.

Back Cover

Mikhail Gorbachev with U.S. Secretary of State George Shultz in the Kremlin.

17 апреля.
Классная работа
Тема урока: Относительная
x=0,256
a=0,25

Esteemed Mr. Prime Minister
Esteemed Mrs. Gandhi,
Dear Indian friends,
Comrades,
We are glad to welcome in Moscow the Prime Minister, and the representatives accompanying him, of a country for which people in the Soviet Union have great respect. Meetings between Soviet and Indian leaders are always marked by warmth and cordiality and a high level of confidence and mutual understanding. They have a beneficial effect on the development of relations between our two countries, on the situation in Asia, and the world as a whole.

Years and decades pass, generations of people in our countries come and go, but the relations of friendship and cooperation between the Soviet Union and India continue to develop favorably. This is happening because these relations are built on the basis of equality and mutual respect, on the coincidence or similarity in the position of the two countries on the cardinal problems of our time.

Our cooperation with India, cooperation which today has so many dimensions, is free of all pressure, of imposition of any terms. The Soviet Union has supported India consistently at all stages of its struggle for stronger independence and has displayed, and continues to display, effective solidarity with the great country that is upholding its sovereignty, its dignity, its right to an independent path of development.

In any sphere of cooperation with India, we, as friends, share with it the best we have. And we feel great satisfaction that economic ties between the Soviet Union and India have helped solve major problems in India's progress—key problems for each concrete historical period—be it the construction of its heavy industry or the development of its fuel-and-power complex. Among our joint projects today are those that, when they are finished, will undoubtedly make a worthy contribution to the development of India's economy and to strengthening its defenses on the threshold of a new century.

The successful space flight by a joint Soviet-Indian crew also testifies to the great effectiveness and, I would say, great potential of our scientific and technical links.

The breadth and variety of cultural exchanges between the two countries reflect the traditions of mutual interest by their peoples in each other's rich cultures and in their spiritual affinity.

But the magnitude of what has already been achieved should not be allowed to blot out the great opportunities that exist for a further advance. A desire for such an advance has been expressed by both sides during today's talks. We are in just the right position to jointly raise our cooperation in many areas to a qualitatively new level.

A special place is held by the Soviet Union's and India's efforts to remove the threat of war and to end the arms race. No one can ignore the fact that friendship and cooperation between our two countries is playing a more and more important and beneficial role in the entire system of international relations. By force of example, these relations are helping assert the principles of peaceful coexistence and work for stronger peace and security for all peoples. These aims are well served by our Treaty of Peace, Friendship and Cooperation.

All peoples strive for peace and progress. None of them wants war. But there are forces that pursue other aims. They do not wish to reckon with the legitimate interests of others and the political realities of today's world. It is these forces, chasing the chimera of military superiority, that have brought the world to the threshold of a new escalation in the arms race, an escalation of unprecedented scale, which threatens to grow into a qualitatively new phase with uncontrollable results.

What, for instance, can be brought to the peoples by the notorious "Star Wars" program that Washington is trying to camouflage and pass off as a "defense initiative"? First of all, greatly increased risk of nuclear war. And, certainly, a sharp reduction in the chances of achieving an accord on matters of disarmament. Additional enormous funds will be thrown into the furnace of the arms race, including the nuclear arms race. Yet these funds could be used in the interests of the peaceful development of humankind and, specifically, to help solve such urgent problems as eliminating poverty and hunger, disease, and illiteracy.

Therefore, the problem of preventing the militarization of space affects the interests of all countries and peoples and leaves no one on the sidelines. We think that before it is too late and before an irreversible situation is created under the cover of soothing statements, all peace-loving states should raise their voice against this new danger.

One of the realities of our world is the appearance in the international arena of dozens of states in Asia, Africa and Latin America, which are striving to overcome the pernicious consequences of colonialism. The overwhelming majority of them follow a policy of nonalignment. The emergence of the nonaligned movement and the fact that it has become a major factor in world politics have occurred in the natural order of things. This nonalignment patently reflects the striving of the newly independent peoples for cooperation with other states on an equal footing, for the recognition of their legitimate rights and interests by others, for the exclusion from international life of domination and claims to hegemony in any form.

In short, the newly independent countries do not want to be regarded any longer as objects for profit making or to have their territory used for installing military bases and strongholds. And these countries can and must be understood. When they are declared spheres of somebody's "vital interests" without so much as being asked their opinion, there can be no question of their interests being taken into account. Those interests are totally ignored.

There is no need to talk much of how gravely dangerous conflicts in different regions of the world are under present conditions. Taking a closer look, it is not hard to see that these conflicts stem, as a rule, from the imperialist powers' attempts to interfere, in some form or other, in the affairs of newly independent countries and to subjugate them to their influence. Precisely herein lie the primary causes for the appearance of many seats of tension in the world, and not in the much discussed "rivalry of the superpowers."

We think that if every permanent member of the UN Security Council assumed an obligation to strictly observe the principles of noninterference, no use of force or threat of force in relations with the countries of these continents and not drawing them into military blocs, this step would help remove seats of tension and would promote a peaceful settlement of a number of conflicts in Asia, Africa, and Latin America. The Soviet Union is prepared to assume such an obligation. This accords fully with the principles of our foreign policy.

The concept of détente came into existence in Europe. Soon it will be ten years since the day when a historic document was signed in Helsinki, a document that summed up what the peoples mean by this significant word. Much of what was built on this basis has been destroyed by icy winds blowing from across the ocean. But many things have remained, survived, sprouted firm roots, and are bringing tangible benefits to the peoples of the world.

In Asia, the problems of peace and security are today no less and, in some areas, even more acute and painful than in Europe. It is understandable, therefore, that a number of new, important, and constructive initiatives on some aspects of the security of the Asian continent and its individual regions have been put forward in recent years. Among the sponsors of these initiatives are the socialist states and members of the nonaligned movement. The Soviet Union and India are in their number.

These proposals remain on the international agenda. Thus the proposal to make the Indian Ocean a peace zone was supported by the UN General Assembly and the nonaligned movement, specifically at its recent conference in New Delhi. Nor can one underestimate the fact that both of the nuclear powers lying on the Asian continent—the Soviet Union and the People's Republic of China—have pledged not to be the first to use nuclear weapons.

Now the question arises: Is it not advisable, considering all these initiatives and, in some measure, Europe's experience, to think of a common, comprehensive approach to the problem of security in Asia and of a possible pooling of efforts by Asian states in this direction? Of course, the way to this is complicated. But neither was the road to Helsinki smooth or even. Here various methods are evidently possible: bilateral talks and multilateral consultations, up to holding an all-Asian forum for an exchange of opinions and a joint search for constructive solutions at some point in the future.

One thing appears indisputable: The peoples of Asia are no less interested in ensuring peace and peaceful cooperation than the peoples of any other continent, and they can do much to achieve this aim.

We think that India, as a great power enjoying much prestige and respect both among Asian countries and throughout the world, can play a very important part in this process.

We greatly appreciate India's contribution to the cause of strengthening peace and international security and, in this respect, to enhancing the role of the nonaligned movement.

The names of the great Indian leaders Jawaharlal Nehru and Indira Gandhi will remain forever in the memory of the peoples, associated inseparably both with the history of India and the history of the national liberation struggle on all continents. They blazed a political course that India has followed. As a result, India has achieved impressive successes in its internal development and in strengthening its international positions. They did much for the rise and development in today's world.

One of the manifestations of the wide recognition of Indira Gandhi's outstanding contribution to the struggle for preserving and strengthening peace is the posthumous award to her of the International Lenin Prize "For the Promotion of Peace Among Nations."

The Soviet people will always remember Jawaharlal Nehru and Indira Gandhi gratefully as firm and consistent supporters of close friendship and cooperation between our two countries, and we highly appreciate, Mr. Prime Minister, the intention you have expressed to carry forward the cause of your illustrious forerunners.

I can assure you that the leaders of the Soviet Union intend to work actively toward further developing and deepening friendly Soviet-Indian relations. A peace-loving and independent India will always meet with understanding and support from the Soviet Union.

Let me express to you our most sincere feelings and wishes. I wish good health to the esteemed Prime Minister of the Republic of

India, Rajiv Gandhi, Mrs. Gandhi and all our Indian friends!

I wish success and prosperity to the great people of India!

May the friendship and cooperation between our countries grow deeper!

May there be lasting peace on earth!

May 21, 1985

18

LUNCHEON
IN THE KREMLIN
IN HONOR OF
WILLY BRANDT

ESTEEMED Mr. Chairman, Esteemed guests, comrades,

May I cordially greet Willy Brandt, leader of the Social Democratic Party of Germany and President of the Socialist International.

We have just had a detailed conversation, and I think we can say honestly that our talk was instructive and useful and has helped us to better understand each other's position.

Our people have a simple but wise saying: "As you sow, so shall you reap." You, Mr. Brandt, sowed in this recent past a good seed in the field of relations between the Soviet Union and the Federal Republic of Germany, in the field of European cooperation. The signing of the historic Moscow Treaty in August 1970 is associated inseparably with your name. That treaty ushered in a period of new, constructive, and truly good-neighborly relations between our two countries and peoples. At the same time, it paved the way to productive cooperation in a broader context between European capitalist and socialist countries or, as they say, between East and West.

Regrettably, the main achievement of those years, détente, though it continues to a considerable extent to bear fruit for the peoples of our continent, has been subject to fierce attack by conservative and reactionary forces. The word itself has been outlawed from the political vocabulary by a number of Western statesmen.

Discussing the international situation today, we have both agreed that there is a good deal in it to deeply worry all who care for world peace and cherish ideals of progress.

Indeed, the threat of war has grown and become more acute during the years of confrontation. The world has approached a very dangerous point. The arms race is being carried on and has reached unprecedented proportions. Moreover, those same forces which have provoked it are now looking up avidly into outer space.

There are no people in the world who are not worried by the U.S. plans to militarize outer space. This worry is well founded.

Let us take a realistic view of matters: the implementation of such plans would thwart the disarmament talks. Moreover, it would increase dramatically the threat of a truly global, destructive military conflict. Anyone capable of an unbiased analysis of the situation and sincerely wishing to safeguard peace cannot but oppose "Star Wars."

Of course, space will always attract man. Space exploration, as we have learned in practice, can do a good deal for the development and improvement of our life on earth. It would be good if states could join efforts in some form and organize cooperation, not to make space a source of death and destruction, but to explore it for peaceful purposes, in the interests of and in accordance with the peaceable requirements of all peoples. The Soviet Union stands for such cooperation.

We have a firm political will for peace, for averting war, and for reducing armaments to the extent of the complete prohibition and elimination of nuclear weapons. This is a will for détente and for establishing normal relations of good-neighborliness and mutual cooperation with all countries, regardless of their social systems. And, as you well know, we are translating this will of ours into constructive initiatives and clear-cut proposals which leave no room for controversial interpretation. It is in this spirit that we are acting at all the current talks in Geneva, Stockholm, and Vienna.

I want to note with satisfaction, Mr. Chairman, that your party, the Social Democratic Party of Germany, plays a prominent role in the struggle for resolving questions of war and peace. This is evidenced by the positions, presented in the documents of the Social Democratic Party of Germany and in your statements, against the "Star Wars" plans and in favor of containing the arms race, reducing armaments, first and foremost nuclear, concluding a treaty between the countries of East and West on the mutual non-use of force, stopping outside interference in the affairs of sovereign countries and peoples, and ending armed conflicts and aggressive ventures in various parts of the world. These views, to which your party and you have arrived by your own ways, following your political convictions, are in many ways consonant with our ideas of the world and the tasks to make it better.

Recently we all fittingly marked the fortieth anniversary of the defeat of Hitler's fascism. That anniversary again reminded us most forcefully of the importance of resolving — without delay — the acute question of ensuring security for the peoples of our continent today. What makes this task even more urgent is the fact that there are forces in the world, including West Germany, which have not learned the lessons of the past war. They hold forth openly and unashamedly on turning Europe into a "theater of operations."

We appreciate highly the firm position of your party, which stands for preventing any new war from being unleashed from German soil. The Soviet Union, as you know, is doing everything possible to really strengthen European security.

We believe that a dependable way to this goal is offered by the complete ridding of our continent of nuclear weapons, both medium-range and tactical, and of chemical weapons. We are fully prepared to resolve the problem in this manner.

Progress in large-scale measures can also be made step by step. Various options for this progress have already been proposed. For instance, what I have in mind are ideas to establish nuclear-free zones in different parts of Europe and the proposal of Mr. Palme, the Swedish Prime Minister, to establish a zone in Europe free from battlefield nuclear weapons. The Soviet Union has already voiced support for the creation of such zones and we have not changed our views. We similarly share and energetically support the idea of your party on the establishment in Europe of a zone free from chemical weapons.

We know well, Mr. Brandt, with what attention you approach the problems of relations between developed and developing nations. We understand this well. Human conscience cannot tolerate the fact that dozens of millions of people in Africa, Asia, and Latin America die from hunger and disease, or live illiterate and impoverished lives. The normal development of newly free countries, the overcoming of the backwardness inherited by them from their colonial past and the establishment of truly equal relations between them and the industrialized capitalist countries are important preconditions for the normalization of international relations as a whole.

The time seems to be coming when the questions of establishing equal international economic relations without any discrimination and of a new international economic order, including the problem of the developing countries' indebtedness, will have to be discussed internationally on a large scale. We support such discussions. The world community has good reason to display concern for the economic security of states and peoples.

Obviously, Mr. Brandt, our views on many current problems are close and even identical in many respects. I think that we come to identical ideas and proposals because we are aware of the gravity of the danger faced by humankind and because our parties sense the mood of the masses who want a lasting peace and who are strongly opposed to policies escalating the threat of nuclear war.

Of course, we have had and will have ideological differences. But they should not interfere with the cooperation of the Communists and the Social Democrats on the most important and acute problems of our day.

Let me express a hope for the successful development of constructive cooperation between our parties, between the CPSU and the Socialist International, in the name of safeguarding peace and security for the peoples.

I wish you, Mr. Brandt, your wife, and the notable Social Democratic leaders who accompany you the best of health and well-being.

May 27, 1985

19

SPEECH
AT THE DINNER
IN HONOR OF
ITALIAN PRIME MINISTER
BETTINO CRAXI

ESTEEMED Mr. Prime Minister,
Esteemed Mrs. Craxi,
Esteemed Italian guests,
Comrades,

We are glad to welcome you to Moscow, esteemed Mr. Craxi, all the more so since it is your first visit to our country in the capacity of the head of the Italian Government. Your visit to the Soviet Union is a clear sign of the desire of both sides to give an additional impetus to Soviet-Italian political contacts. We value the fact that mutually beneficial relations have been established and are developing effectively in various fields between the Soviet Union and Italy.

On more than one occasion in Western Europe, Italian statesmen displayed farsightedness and a well-balanced approach, and initiated substantial moves to improve East-West relations. Nor have we forgotten the major, bold, and enterprising actions in trade and economy which continue to be symbolized by the huge plant in Togliatti on the Volga River.

Neither you nor we are closing our eyes to the fact that there are differences between the Soviet Union and Italy on certain — and quite substantial — international problems. It is important, however, that there is an obvious mutual desire for a constructive dialogue and for a joint search for ways to lessen today's dangerous tensions.

There is indeed a need for action here. The world is living through difficult times. The hopes which the peoples justifiably pinned on the process of positive changes in international relations, initiated through the efforts of many countries during the 1970s, have not been met, for reasons which we have pointed out on more than one occasion. That process was superseded by confrontation, the mentality of which is spurring on the arms race which has gone too far as it is. In certain quarters, an arms buildup with a view to breaking the existing military-strategic balance has, in turn, been breeding a dangerous fondness for methods and means of aggression in foreign policy. This vicious circle — confrontation-arms race-confrontation—can and must be broken. Human civilization simply does not have any choice.

Italy—and, of course, not only Italy—can be sure of the Soviet Union's policy. Our people, who paid a great price for the right to live in peace and freedom, are devoting every effort to peaceful construction, to the acceleration of scientific and technical progress, and to raising the material and cultural standards of life.

I say this to emphasize that the Soviet Union's desire for peace is determined by the very nature of our social system, by our world outlook, and by our morality. Our thoughts are turning back to the experience accumulated during the 1970s precisely because at that time good political, legal, moral, and psychological foundations were laid for peaceful cooperation among states with different social systems and different military-political alliances. We want to revive the spirit, the atmosphere and the essence of détente precisely because we intend to advance even farther toward a dependable system of international law and order and security. A qualitative leap is needed.

At the Soviet-American talks in Geneva, the second round of which begins tomorrow, the Soviet Union is prepared to seek mutually acceptable solutions in a businesslike manner. Regrettably, so far, we have not sensed sufficient readiness in our partners in the talks. There are many indications that the United States would like to push through its plans to develop armaments of a new class, space-based strike arms at all costs. The price of this, however, may go beyond the subversion of the Geneva talks to ruin every prospect of an end to the arms race.

We in the Soviet Union follow a different logic. Outer space, a common asset of humankind, must not become a scene of military rivalry. If outer space is not militarized, it will be possible to reduce substantially both strategic nuclear armaments and medium-range nuclear systems in Europe.

Naturally, the question of European-based systems has a special place in our exchange of opinions. I want to emphasize most definitely that we are prepared to travel a long road in that matter. The proposals made by us still stand.

If they are put into practice, there will be the lowest possible level of all – a zero level – in the increase of medium-range missiles in Europe between the Soviet Union and the United States. As for the medium-range missiles we retain in the European zone, we would not have a grain more than the French and the British have either in missile or in warhead numbers. We are prepared to scrap the missiles subject to removal without redeploying them anywhere.

Let me also point out that the Soviet Union has long stated that if an agreement on the limitation of nuclear armaments in Europe is achieved and enters into force, the deployment of SS-20 missiles in the eastern parts of the Soviet Union will also be stopped on the condition that there will be no substantial changes in the strategic situation in Asia. We are reiterating this proposal today.

As for Europe, we state over and over again: the Soviet Union wants, most of all, the complete ridding on that continent of both medium-range and tactical nuclear weapons – that is, weapons intended to hit targets in Europe. The Soviet Union has long been prepared for this, but the NATO countries prefer pretending that they do not hear our proposal.

Elementary logic tells us that to turn around the arms race, it is first necessary to halt it. In order to facilitate the move to arms reductions, the Soviet Union has proposed a freeze on the development of space-based strike arms, on strategic offensive armaments and on medium-range nuclear systems for the duration of the Soviet-American talks in Geneva. To get things off to a good start, we unilaterally suspended the deployment of our medium-range systems in Europe until November. We are still awaiting a response from the other side to this initiative, one that would contribute toward accomplishing the task of scaling down nuclear confrontation in Europe.

To sum up, I would like to stress that the implementation of the Soviet Union's clear, concrete and far-reaching proposals would certainly change the entire situation in Europe and in the world radically for the better. We are sure that Italy, along with other nations, could contribute a good deal to such a development.

Continuing the subject of strengthening European security, I want to say that we seem to have with Italy a certain similarity of approach to proceedings at the Stockholm Conference. We stand for the early beginning of substantive talks and for the formulation of relevant documents at the conference. It is evidently necessary to look more boldly for an accord incorporating major political measures and mutually acceptable and concrete confidence-building measures in military matters.

We think that the tenth anniversary of the signing of the Helsinki Final Act, which will be marked on August 1 this year, should be keynoted by the restoration and expansion of the process of détente. The historical importance of that document, pervaded as it is with the spirit of détente, should be backed in joint action by the participating states. And, of course, attempts under whatever pretext to erode the territorial and political realities in Europe should be blocked resolutely. It would be unpardonable thoughtlessness to disregard the fact that it was precisely the postwar setup in Europe that has given the continent forty years of peace.

I will touch upon one more aspect of European affairs. Europe is a continent where there are various multilateral organizations. Each of them has accumulated a wealth of experience and is playing a specific role both in the world economy and in international politics. I mean primarily the Council for Mutual Economic Assistance and the European Economic Community. It is time, I think, to establish between them mutually beneficial relations in economic affairs. Insofar as the EEC countries act as a "political entity," we are prepared to seek with it a common language on concrete international problems.

Mr. Prime Minister,

It is natural that in the course of our talk today, reviewing the over-all international situation, we could not help touching upon seats of acute tension in the world, be it the Mediterranean or Central America. And I think that the Soviet Union and Italy have a certain similarity of approach here. These dangerous seats of tension should be removed by political means. We stand for continued efforts to bring positions closer, for more energetic assistance to a search for ways to settle regional problems at the negotiating table, and for protection of the sovereign rights of states and peoples exposed to pressure and gross intervention in their internal affairs.

Relations between the Soviet Union and Italy have a substantive legal base. During the past decades, the sides have perfected mechanisms and instruments of cooperation, such as the 1972 Protocol on consultations and a number of bilateral documents on economic, scientific, technical, and cultural exchanges. Perhaps we can learn to use these instruments even more efficiently for the good of both sides and for peace and security for all peoples. We are prepared to contribute to such efforts. In this context, we reiterate our satisfaction with your visit to the Soviet Union, with the intensive exchange of opinions we just had.

I am certain that, basing ourselves on the long-time sentiments of mutual respect and affection between the Soviet and Italian peoples, we can still do a good number of useful things by our joint efforts for the further development of Soviet Italian relations.

Allow me, Mr. Prime Minister, to wish you, your esteemed wife, Foreign Minister Andreotti, and all the other Italian guests the best of health and well-being.

May Soviet-Italian relations develop and grow stronger for the good of our peoples and the cause of world peace!

May 29, 1985

20

SPEECH
AT THE DINNER
IN HONOR OF
GUSTÁV HUSÁK

DEAR Comrade Husák,
Dear Czechoslovakian friends,
Comrades,
The official friendship visit to our country by the leader of fraternal Czechoslovakia is drawing to a close. Briefly summarizing the results of the visit, we may say that another important step has been taken in the development of Soviet-Czechoslovak cooperation and in the strengthening of friendship and relations of alliance between our parties and peoples.

All of us are sincerely glad to have this new meeting with Comrade Husák, a prominent leader in the international communist movement and a long-time and loyal friend of our country. Recently the Federal Assembly of Czechoslovakia reelected him President of the Republic. I would like to congratulate you cordially once again, dear Comrade Husák, and wish you the best of health and success in your important party and state work.

Comrades, at the beginning of May, we festively celebrated the anniversary of the great victory over fascism and simultaneously the fortieth anniversary of the completion of the national liberation struggle of the Czechs and Slovaks and the liberation of your country from the nazi invaders. All the subsequent development of Czechoslovakia has been continuously associated with those historic events.

A good demonstration of this fact is the national jubilee exhibition Czechoslovakia-1985, which opened today in Moscow. It is an impressive account of the results of the road traveled by the country, a sort of report by the people's rule about the transformations carried out, and clear evidence of the superiority of the socialist system and its boundless potentialities. At the same time, it is a marvelous example of how greatly socialist countries benefit by cooperation and mutual assistance and of what they can accomplish by pooling their efforts.

While the exhibition makes it possible to evaluate present achievements, the program for long-term economic, scientific, and technical cooperation between the Soviet Union and Czechoslovakia signed by us for the period up to the year 2000 offers a glimpse of the future. It defines guidelines for our economic cooperation and major joint projects which will be important to the national economies of both countries.

Economic ties between the Soviet Union and Czechoslovakia have reached considerable proportions. The Soviet Union has long been Czechoslovakia's leading trade partner, while Czechoslovakia is our country's second largest. We must now go much farther. I am referring to the development of those areas of our cooperation which offer the greatest return, namely, specialization and cooperation in engineering and other industries.

Clear prospects and confidence for the future are immensely important in today's world with its complicated conditions for economic growth, dramatic market fluctuations, and tough competition. It is these prospects and this confidence that the fraternal countries gain through socialist economic integration and through their cooperation on a bilateral and multilateral basis within the CMEA framework. But that boon does not lie on the surface. One must work well to make good use of it. A good deal remains to be done and a number of major problems must be resolved together.

The priority is to work jointly in accelerating scientific and technical progress. Today this is the key to intensifying social production, to raising the living standards of the population and to improving the entire socialist way of life and, of course, to strengthening the defense capability of the socialist countries.

Another important task is to find the optimal and most efficient mechanism of cooperation among the CMEA member countries and to introduce economic forms and methods that would stimulate the pooling of efforts in material production, scientific research and design, and experimental work.

Understandably, both problems — advance to the foremost frontiers of science and technology, and the development of an even more flexible and efficient mechanism of economic cooperation — are closely interrelated. All the fraternal countries are interested in solving these problems. In the course of our talks today, both sides reiterated the determination of the Soviet Union and Czechoslovakia, along with the other CMEA members, to make a fitting contribution to that vitally important cause.

We are convinced that the rise to higher levels of economic integration will mean a new quality of cooperation among fraternal countries in all other spheres as well. On more than one occasion, Lenin pointed out the interdependence of economics and politics. Practice constantly proves the correctness of this idea. The current objective processes of social development necessitate the need to expand the international socialist division of labor and to strengthen the unity and cohesion of the peoples following the road of socialism.

We cannot close our eyes to realities. Regrettably, the world situation remains complex and dangerous. American first-strike nuclear missiles continue to be deployed in Western Europe. West German revanchism is again making itself heard; the decisions of the Yalta and Potsdam conferences of the Allied powers and the results of the postwar development are called into question, with obvious encouragement from across the ocean.

The actions of the aggressive imperialist forces in various parts of the world, their enroachment upon the norms of international law and their disregard of world public opinion are deplorable.

The Soviet Union and Czechoslovakia, along with other fraternal countries, have stood consistently for ending the escalation of tension created by imperialism, which could lead to nuclear conflict, and are working painstakingly for the solution of urgent problems.

Our clear position and initiatives concerning this are well known. We proposed to the United States at the Geneva talks to take joint measures to prevent the militarization of space and to terminate the arms race on earth. This would be immensely important to reducing and eventually eliminating the threat of war.

The second round of those talks opened in Geneva yesterday. As before, the Soviet Union will work at these talks for honest and fair decisions in strict accordance with the principle of equality and equal security. Naturally, we need reciprocity in this matter of vital importance.

The Soviet Union reiterates its proposal for an immediate

moratorium on nuclear and space weapons. Such a moratorium
would curb the arms race on earth and prevent its extension to outer
space and nuclear weapons would not give advantage to either side,
but would fully meet the principle of equality and equal security.

The introduction of a moratorium is viewed by us as just the
first step which can help strengthen mutual trust and proceed onto
the road of significant reductions in nuclear armaments. We suggest
that in introducing the moratorium, the Soviet Union and the United
states agree that they will suggest practical proposals at the talks
within a specified period—say, a month or two—on all matters
under consideration, including the levels to which they would be
prepared to reduce their strategic offensive armaments—naturally,
on the condition that space-strike weapons are banned.

We stand for returning Soviet-American relations to normalcy,
to the road of détente and mutually beneficial cooperation. It is time
for the American side to translate its statements of readiness to
move in that direction into the language of practical actions.

I would like to stress with satisfaction that we and our Czechoslovakian friends have a common approach to urgent international
problems. We draw on unity for strength. The Warsaw Treaty
Organization has been ensuring our countries' security and the
possibility to live and work in conditions of peace for three decades.
Recently it was decided unanimously to extend the treaty. We shall
continue to perfect and strengthen our defensive military and political alliance.

Comrades, Soviet and Czechoslovakian Communists are now
preparing for the regular congresses of their parties. The period
before the congress, as usual, involves the summing up of results,
the identification of reserves, and the formulation of tasks for the
future. The most important of those tasks is the strengthening of
friendship between allied socialist states, our associates in the
struggle to achieve common goals.

Friendship among the peoples of the socialist countries is the
greatest achievement, one might say; our common priceless asset
that we should preserve and replenish.

Let us then continue to do everything possible to strengthen
comprehensive interaction between our fraternal parties and to

expand relations of comradeship and friendship between the Soviet and Czechoslovak peoples.

Let us continue to resolutely strive for a common cause: socialism and peace.

In conclusion, allow me to speak on behalf of the Soviet leadership, on behalf of our entire party and the Soviet people, to wish Comrade Husák, the leaders of the Communist Party of Czechoslovakia, and all the Communists and working people of fraternal Czechoslovakia, continued success in striving for the good of their socialist homeland.

May 31, 1985

21

FROM THE SPEECH AT THE DNEPROPETROVSK FACTORY

THE SOVIET PEOPLE know well the enormous efforts made by our Party and government to uphold peace, to save the earth from a nuclear catastrophe. In his day, Lenin expressed the principled position of the socialist state clearly, saying: "We promise the workers and peasants to do all we can for peace . . . this we shall do."

Many years have passed since then. Our people have lived through hard years, through the bloodiest wars. Our state has become stronger and mightier with every passing year. Today we are a great world power which is ready to repel any aggressor. But today we promise workers and farmers to do more than ever before for peace. And we shall do this.

We live in tense times. You can see this. The life and death of hundreds of millions of people, the destiny of all mankind depends on whether the instigators of war will be stopped.

In present conditions, as we deal with the problems of strengthening international peace, we should, in the first place, consolidate the positions of socialist countries in the world arena, contribute to all-around cooperation between them. We are working toward this. I mean the expansion of economic cooperation and the economic integration of the member countries of the Council for Mutual Economic Assistance. Well-organized specialization and production cooperation, and vigorous interaction in developing science and technology make our whole community, and every member, stronger economically and stronger in the defense capability. They bring to naught the policy of economic pressure which is now being actively pursued by the West toward socialist countries.

The extension of the Warsaw Treaty this April—the political and defense basis of our fraternal alliance—for the next twenty years is an important event. This extension enables us to be still more active in our joint struggle for peace. On the whole, it should be pointed out, comrades, that the relations between the socialist-community countries are becoming closer and deeper, and contacts between their political leaders more fruitful. This is a great achievement. We shall spare no effort to encourage this process.

I have already had an opportunity to speak about our relations with the People's Republic of China. I think that time has shown both sides that neither China nor the Soviet Union benefit from estrangement and even less from unfriendliness and suspicion, and that good-neighborly cooperation is possible and desirable. For our part, we are going to work vigorously so that the negative period in Soviet-Chinese relations, which gave rise to many artificial problems, should be overcome fully. I am sure that eventually this will be achieved.

The current world situation is characterized by the ever-growing role in the international arena of countries which have recently freed themselves from colonial or semicolonial dependence and have embarked on the road of independent development. Much in world development will depend on the destiny of these countries and of how more developed states will build relations with them.

This question is absolutely clear for the Soviet Union. We regard the peoples who have liberated themselves from colonialism as our friends and equal partners in the struggle for peace and progress, support their striving to consolidate their sovereignty fully and defend their freedom and independence. Within the framework of equal cooperation, we are doing all we can to assist them in establishing advanced national economies of their own.

In a word, we are and will be doing everything to expand and deepen our equal and friendly cooperation with newly free countries. This expanded relationship has also been the goal of our recent meetings and talks with the leaders of such countries as India, Syria and Nicaragua. We regard an alliance of the forces of social progress and national liberation as a guarantee of mankind's better future.

The imperialist countries are pursuing policies that are different in principle. For ages they have been exploiting labor in the colonies, plundering their natural resources, and keeping their peoples in poverty. These days, too, attempts are being made to tie those peoples to the capitalist system, using economic and military means, threats and intimidation, handouts and bribes. Many of these countries are caught in the noose of foreign debt, which is being drawn ever tighter. The newly free states are being told which policies to pursue at home. People who disagree or disobey are overthrown and assassinated. This is the common practice of the "free world" states, which are pursuing colonialist policies.

Aggressive capitalist forces are unwilling to recognize in practice the right of all states to sovereignty, independence and the free determination of the ways of their development. These forces attempt to impose their will on these countries and try to recarve and change the modern world in their own way at all costs. This is the major source of danger for nations at present, the biggest threat to universal peace.

The greatest problem today is that of ending the arms race, which has swept the world, and of reducing existing stockpiles. In principle, we need no nuclear or other weapons to build normal relations with the capitalist world if it renounces its aggressive plans against the Soviet Union and other socialist countries.

We are prepared to compete with capitalism exclusively in peaceful creative activities. Therefore, we are for the development of political dialogue and interaction with capitalist states, for the large-scale development of mutually beneficial trade, economic, scientific, technical and cultural relations, and are ready to develop such relations on a stable long-term basis. But these relations must be honest and genuinely mutually advantageous, without any discrimination. Attempts to use trade as a tool for interfering in our domestic affairs are futile. We do not need such trade. We can do without it.

We are ready for talks not only on ending the arms race, but on the greatest possible arms reductions, up to general and complete disarmament. As you know, our talks with the United States are currently under way in Geneva. Their goal, as the Soviet leadership sees it, is to stop the arms race on earth and prevent it in outer space. We have agreed to hold the talks because we want such goals to be achieved in practice. But, by all appearances, this is the very thing the U.S. Administration and the military-industrial complex which it serves do not want. They do not seem to be willing of achieving serious agreements. They continue implementing a huge program for the accelerated development of ever-new weapons of mass destruction in the hope of achieving superiority over the socialist countries and of dictating their own will to these states.

Not only have the Americans failed to put forward any serious proposals in Geneva for slowing down the arms race but, on the contrary, they have been taking steps to make it impossible. I refer to the so-called "Star Wars" program, to create space-based strike weapons. Claims about its "defensive" character are tales for naïve people. Their idea is to try to paralyze the strategic arms of the Soviet Union and to get a chance to carry out a nuclear strike against our country with impunity.

That is the essence of the matter which we cannot but take into account. The Soviet Union, should it be faced with a real threat from space, would find an effective way to counter it—let no one doubt that. I say it quite definitely. So far one thing is clear: The American space militarization program is a solid wall barring the way to appropriate accords in Geneva.

By its militaristic policy, the U.S. Administration is making itself heavily responsible before humanity. Let me add that should it resolve to take up a more sensible stand, there would be a prospect for a mutually acceptable agreement on far-reaching, really deep cuts in nuclear-arms stockpiles by both sides. There would be a way to scrap these weapons altogether and remove the threat of nuclear war, which is what all the peoples of the earth are dreaming about.

But if our partners at the Geneva talks should stick to their stalling tactics at the meetings of the delegations, to dodging the solutions they have assembled for while speeding up their military programs—in space, on earth, and at sea—we would naturally have to reappraise the whole situation. We just cannot let the talks be used again for pulling the wool over people's eyes and covering up military preparations with the object of securing U.S. strategic superiority and world domination. I am sure our opposition to these designs will be supported by the real forces of peace all over the world, and we are supported by the Soviet people.

The Party's Central Committee notes with great satisfaction that our peace-oriented foreign policy has the full understanding and approval of the Soviet people. The main point is that not only do the Soviet people approve of it, but they are backing it up with what they do, with their work. The more effective this work is, the richer and stronger our country is, the greater will be its contribution to world peace and the progress of humanity.

June 26, 1985

22

SPEECH
IN HONOR OF
LE DUAN
AND
HIS DELEGATION

DEAR Comrade Le Duan,
Dear Vietnamese friends,
Comrades,

It is with great satisfaction that we welcome the visit to our country by a party and government delegation from the Socialist Republic of Vietnam, led by Comrade Le Duan, General Secretary of the Central Committee of the Communist Party of Vietnam. We are convinced that the visit will mark another important step in the overall development and strengthening of Soviet-Vietnamese brotherhood and cooperation.

Soviet-Vietnamese friendship has deep roots and solid traditions. President Ho Chi Minh, a great son of the Vietnamese people and a great friend of our country, was close to the source of this friendship. It has stood the test of time and been tempered both in the grim years of war and in the everyday life of peace.

The people of the Soviet Union and Vietnam are marching hand in hand, tackling the tasks of building socialism and communism jointly and upholding the cause of peace and international security.

We have held thorough and intense talks. As before, they were marked by a cordial, truly comradely atmosphere. Both in the Soviet Union and in Vietnam work has got under way on a large scale now to prepare for the 27th Congress of the CPSU and the 6th Congress of the CPV. This agenda lends special political significance to our exchange of opinions.

I think we should be gladdened by the development of Soviet-Vietnamese relations. They are based on the reliable foundation of the Treaty of Friendship and Cooperation and have now reached a high level and become an inalienable part of the social life of our two countries.

Much attention was paid to economic cooperation in the course of our conversations. The Soviet Union and Vietnam wish to tap even more actively the considerable potentialities they have to deepen their interaction in this field and make it more effective. We are positive that our shared political will can be fully embodied in implementing practical measures to jointly carry out the long-term program for developing economic, scientific and technological cooperation between the Soviet Union and Vietnam and in coordinating our plans for national economic development for 1986-1990.

The problems of scientific and technological progress figured prominently in the negotiations. Both sides are sure that it is only along these lines that it is possible to accomplish social and economic tasks consistently and to consolidate the positions of socialism still further. Each fraternal socialist country is making a contribution of its own to the fulfillment of these strategic tasks.

The talks confirmed that the fraternal links between the Soviet Union and Vietnam rest on the firm, tested foundation of Marxism-Leninism and socialist internationalism, and meet the fundamental interests and aspirations of our people, the interests of world peace.

Comrades,

This year the people of our countries, all progressive people on the earth direct their thoughts again and again to the fortieth anniversary of the great victory over German fascism and Japanese militarism.

The lessons of World War II remind mankind of how important and how vital peace is. The value of peace is especially great now that another world war would spell disaster for humanity. This is why it is so imperative to take urgent and effective measures to remove the nuclear threat from the life of present and future generations, to prevent the extension of the arms race to outer space and stop it on the earth, and to turn international relations in the direction of equitable and mutually advantageous cooperation.

The foreign policy of the Soviet Union and other states of the socialist community, their ideas and proposals, the broad package of their peace initiatives have been dictated by concern for preserving peace on the earth. Peaceful coexistence, the equal and reliable security of all sides, the lowering of the levels of military confrontation and of world military-political tension as a whole, and the prevention of hegemonism in any form — this is what we want and what we are seeking to secure.

A great contribution to improving the state of the world would undoubtedly be made if a political awareness of the acute need to move toward normalizing the situation prevailed in the world's largest and most populous part, namely Asia and the Pacific basin. So far, regrettably, it has not.

One cannot but see that the United States has of late stepped up its military preparations markedly in that region. It is encouraging revanchist trends in the policy of Japan's ruling circles and pursuing the attempt to forge a militarist alliance involving Washington, Tokyo and Seoul. Washington is busy trying to enlist the countries of the region in implementing its global military-political plans, including the notorious "Pacific Doctrine." It is interfering in the affairs of sovereign nations and obstructing the settling of problems by negotiations. The cutting edge of this policy is directed against the Soviet Union, Vietnam and other socialist states in Asia, against Afghanistan and Kampuchea. But, by its very essence, this policy threatens all nations in the Asian-Pacific region.

Naturally enough, such actions which endanger peace cannot but cause concern among the countries of that region and, at times, force them to take legitimate countermeasures.

The Soviet Union's policy meets the desire of nations for peace and cooperation. We support the culmination of points of conflict and oppose the imperialist policy that leads to a further dangerous destabilization of the situation.

Our country is prepared resolutely to cut the knots which have not been tied by us. For example, we are for reducing the level of confrontation in medium-range nuclear systems. We have declared on more than one occasion that should a corresponding agreement be reached in Europe, we shall scrap the number of medium-range missiles in the European part of the country, on which the agreement will have been reached. We have also stated our consent to freeze the number of missiles in the Asian part of the Soviet Union on condition that the American side does not take steps toward changing the strategic situation in the region. The Soviet Union would not oppose the discussion of this problem with Asian and Pacific states having similar systems, with a view to limiting and subsequently reducing these systems — on the basis of reciprocity, of course.

Recently we have put forward the idea of holding a Pan-Asian forum to exchange opinions and jointly look for constructive solutions. The first responses to this proposal have indicated that a desire for such an exchange of opinions exists. Certainly, there are difficulties as well. Not all people like such a vigorous posing of the issue. There are forces that have received the idea with hostility. But we have no lack of goodwill, patience, and persistence. We call on all interested countries on the continent to display supreme political wisdom and to begin in earnest to tackle the fundamental problems of strengthening peace and security.

We are convinced that Asia can and should become a continent of peace and good-neighborliness. It is only in conditions of genuine peace and stability that the countries of the region can accomplish the difficult tasks of social and economic development facing them successfully.

This is the goal of the specific proposals of the Soviet Union, the countries of Indochina and other socialist countries, including the proposals for working out confidence-building measures in the Far East and concluding a convention on mutual nonaggression and non-use of force in relations between the states of Asia and the Pacific. The initiatives of India and a number of other nonaligned countries have the same goal as these proposals.

Normalization of the relations of the Soviet Union and Vietnam with the People's Republic of China would undoubtedly help fortify the foundations of peace in Asia and outside it. Both the Soviet Government and the Vietnamese government have already made constructive proposals in this respect. A positive response to them could help remove many of the existing obstacles in the way of good-neighborly and mutually beneficial relations in the region.

The Soviet Union believes, as before, that there are no problems in Southeast Asia that cannot be settled politically at the negotiating table. That is why we fully support the consistent efforts undertaken by Vietnam, jointly with Laos and Kampuchea, to establish relations of good-neighborliness and cooperation in Southeast Asia and turn the region into a zone of peace and stability. The Soviet Union will continue promoting any steps in this direction in every way.

Comrades,

The day is not far off when the working people of Vietnam will mark the fortieth anniversary of Southeast Asia's first state of workers and peasants. The Soviet people see this glorious anniversary as a big holiday of their own. It is highly symbolic that in anticipation of this great date it has been decided to erect a monument in Moscow to the patriot and internationalist Ho Chi Minh, founder of the Communist Party of Vietnam and the Vietnamese socialist state.

The Soviet people have always displayed solidarity with fraternal Vietnam and given it all-around support and assistance. The Vietnamese Communists and all working people in Vietnam may be confident that the cause of building socialism on Vietnamese soil, the cause of Vietnam's freedom and independence will continue to have a firm support in our solidarity. The policy of strengthening Soviet-Vietnamese friendship and cooperation is a policy of principle of our Party and country.

Permit me to express the wish to the Communists and all working people of Vietnam who are guided by their tested vanguard, the Communist Party of Vietnam, to mark the forthcoming sixth Congress of the CPV in a fitting manner and achieve fresh successes in building a powerful and flourishing Vietnam, a reliable outpost of socialism in Asia.

I wish sound health and successes to Comrade Le Duan, General Secretary of the CPV Central Committee, to the members of the Communist Party of Vietnam and government delegation and to all Vietnamese and Soviet comrades present here.

Let indestructible Soviet-Vietnamese friendship develop and grow ever stronger!

June 28, 1985

23

SPEECH
AT THE SESSION
OF THE
SUPREME SOVIET
OF THE USSR

COMRADE Deputies,

We now have to elect the President of the Presidium of the Supreme Soviet of the USSR.

The Plenary Meeting of the CPSU Central Committee held yesterday discussed this question.

As you are aware, beginning with 1977, the General Secretary of the CPSU Central Committee has occupied simultaneously both his own post and that of President of the Presidium of the Supreme Soviet of the USSR. It must be said that in the conditions of the time, the combination in one person of the two highest posts within the Party and the state was justified. In that period, the legislative and other activities of the USSR Supreme Soviet were stepped up, the work of the local Soviets was improved, and control over the organs of administration was strengthened.

At the same time, the Central Committee took into account that the performance of the new tasks which are now facing us demands the correction of both the meaning and the form and methods of Party and state activities, and of the placing of personnel both in the center and locally.

The country is now living through a responsible period. We are determining the strategic course for the near and distant future and are elaborating a draft for the new edition of the Party Program that is to be adopted by the 27th CPSU Congress. An entire complex of important tasks faces us. You know them. It is the transfer of the economy to intensive development: the structural reconstruction of production; the introduction of effective forms of labor management, organization and stimulation; the further raising of the Soviet people's well-being; and strengthening the country's defense capacity.

Today, when we see our prospects better, it is the organizational work, the stepping up of the activities of all the links in the Soviet political system and the mobilization of the masses in performing the tasks posed that have moved to the forefront. All this presupposes the further strengthening of the Party's guiding role in society and calls for the intensification of the work done by the CPSU Central Committee and its Politburo.

The CPSU Central Committee has deemed it expedient in these concrete conditions, and taking into account the tasks of the current stage, for the General Secretary of the CPSU Central Committee to concentrate maximally on organizing the work of the Party's central organs and on pooling the efforts of all Party, state and public organizations for the successful implementation of the planned course.

In this connection, the CPSU Central Committee, the Presidium of the Supreme Soviet of the USSR and the Party group of the Supreme Soviet have authorized me to submit for your consideration the proposal, supported by the council of the elders of the chambers, to elect Comrade Andrei Andreyevich Gromyko, President of the Presidium of the Supreme Soviet of the USSR.

The name of Andrei Andreyevich is widely known both in our country and beyond its borders. An outstanding politician, one of the oldest Party members, he contributes greatly to drafting and executing our internal and foreign policy. Profound knowledge and all-round experience are combined in him with an adherence to principle and a consistency in fulfilling the policy elaborated by us. The Party and the people highly appreciate his services in the implementation of the Soviet state's foreign policy. I think that we have every reason to believe that Andrei Andreyevich Gromyko will fulfill the functions connected with administering the work of the Presidium of the Supreme Soviet of the USSR.

As the July Plenary Meeting of the CPSU Central Committee pointed out, the Party, as before, will continue stepping up the activities of the Supreme Soviet, raising the role of the Soviets and strengthening their responsibility for the state of affairs in all fields, in every town and village. They must naturally combine the functions of adopting state decisions with the organization of their fulfillment and control over the implementation of these decisions.

We are stressing over and over again that the Soviets at all stages are called upon to make a much fuller and more consistent use of their rights. They should keep abreast of all fields of social life. Special attention should be given now to the satisfaction of the

working people's varied needs and requirements. It is necessary that
the Soviets do even more for the fulfillment of the Food Program, to
solve the problem of better supplying the population in each republic, territory and region with food products through the mobilization
of local possibilities and reserves. It is important that the Soviets
join wholeheartedly in the organization of consumer-goods production by all industrial enterprises, irrespective of their departmental
subordination. The Soviets, both central and local, must exert even
more effort to solve social problems, satisfy the Soviet people's
cultural requirements, and educate the working people.

We must make better use of the constitutional authority and the
broad practical possibilities available to the USSR Supreme Soviet
in dealing with key questions in the country's life and controlling the
organs of administration. The Supreme Soviet will have to perform
many tasks in improving existing legislation. Durable legality is an
inalienable part of socialist democracy and of the strict adherence to
the principle of social justice. Today, as never before, our society's
life is characterized by the political activity of the Soviet people,
who make many proposals on questions of policy, economy and
other fields of society's life and who react sharply to any shortcomings. This is the real expression of genuine democracy, the expression which we call the socialist people's self-government.

Therefore, we still have much to do to improve the Soviets'
work and to strengthen legality. The role of the Presidium of the
Supreme Soviet and its President should be weighty and active.

Taking all that into account, I put forward for your consideration, Comrade Deputies, the following draft resolution.

"The Supreme Soviet of the Union of Soviet Socialist Republics
resolves:

"To elect Deputy Andrei Andreyevich Gromyko President of
the Presidium of the Supreme Soviet of the USSR.

"At the same time it is proposed to adopt a resolution relieving
Comrade A. A. Gromyko from his duties as First Vice-Chairman of
the Council of Ministers and Minister of Foreign Affairs of the
Soviet Union."

July 2, 1985

24

REPLY
TO THE UNION OF
CONCERNED SCIENTISTS

Dear Mr. Kendall,

I have received the message sent by you on behalf of the Union of Concerned Scientists calling for a ban on space weapons. I want to say that I deeply respect the opinion of prominent scientists who are more keenly aware than many others of what dangerous consequences for mankind the spreading of the arms race to outer space and the conversion of space into an arena of military rivalry could have.

The Union of Concerned Scientists has every grounds to demand that a clear and irrevocable political decision be made which would prevent militarization of outer space and leave it free for peaceful cooperation. This issue indeed requires a bold approach. The standards of yesterday, and narrow, moreover illusory, notions, of one-sided benefits and advantages are not applicable here. What is needed now as never before is a farsighted policy based on understanding of the realities and the dangers which we shall inevitably encounter tomorrow, if today those who can and must make the only correct decision evade the responsibility that rests with them.

On behalf of the Soviet leadership I want to make it quite clear that the Soviet Union will not be the first to step into space with weapons. We shall make every effort to convince other countries, and above all the United States of America, not to take such a fatal step which would inevitably increase the threat of nuclear war and spark off an uncontrolled arms race in all areas.

Proceeding from this goal, the Soviet Union, as you evidently know, has submitted a radical proposal to the United Nations — a draft treaty on the prohibition of the use of force in space with regard to earth. If the United States joined the vast majority of states that have supported this initiative, the issue of space weapons could be closed once and for all.

At the Soviet-American talks on nuclear and space arms in Geneva, we are trying to reach agreement on a full ban on the development, testing and deployment of space-based strike systems. Such a ban would make it possible to preserve space for peaceful development, research and scientific discoveries, and moreover, to start the process of sharply reducing and ultimately scrapping nuclear weapons.

We have also repeatedly taken unilateral steps intended to set a good example for the United States. For two years now the moratorium introduced by the Soviet Union on the placement of antisatellite weapons in outer space has been operative, and it will continue to remain in force as long as other states do likewise. Lying on the table in Washington is our proposal that both sides terminate completely all work on the development of new antisatellite systems and that such systems as the Soviet Union and the United States already possess (including those still undergoing tests) be eliminated. The actions of the American side in the near future will show which decision the U.S. Administration will prefer.

Strategic stability and trust would clearly be strengthened if the United States agreed together with the Soviet Union to reaffirm in binding form their commitment to the provisions of the Treaty on the Limitation of Anti-Ballistic Missile Systems, a treaty of unlimited duration. The Soviet Union is not developing strike space weapons or a large-scale ABM system. Nor is it laying the foundation for such a system. It abides strictly by its obligations under the treaty as a whole and in its particular aspects, and observes unswervingly the spirit and the letter of that highly important document. We invite the American leaders to join us in this goal and to renounce plans for space militarization now in the making, plans that would inevitably lead to the negation of that document, which is the key link in the entire process of nuclear arms limitation.

The Soviet Union proceeds from the premise that the practical fulfillment of the task of preventing an arms race in space and terminating it on earth is possible, given the political will and a sincere desire by both sides to work toward this historic goal. The Soviet Union has that desire and that will.

I wish the Union of Concerned Scientists and all its members success in the noble work they are doing for the good of peace and progress.

Yours respectfully,

Mikhail Gorbachev

July 5, 1985

Note: The Union of Concerned Scientists was awarded the Nobel Peace Prize for 1985.

25

SPEECH AT THE OPENING CEREMONY OF THE 12th WORLD FESTIVAL OF YOUTH AND STUDENTS

Dear friends,
Esteemed Guests,

On behalf of the people of our country I hail you in the capital of the Union of Soviet Socialist Republics—Moscow. I congratulate you on the opening of the Twelfth World Festival of Youth and Students.

Such festivals are always a grand occasion, a major international event. An occasion because young envoys from all the continents, people with different world outlooks and national traditions come together. They meet in order to share all the best accumulated in the spiritual treasure-house of every nation and in doing so pave the shortest way toward mutual understanding and friendship. Soviet people are sincerely glad to host this meeting. Their hearts are open to you.

But, naturally, festivals are not only a festive occasion. The problems of life affect and concern young people no less intensely than the senior generations. With the inherent enthusiasm of youth they rise to the battle for social justice and genuine freedom, for making the boons of the world, the boons of civilization accessible to all, for banishing violence and racism, inequality and oppression, militarism and aggression from the life of humanity.

The world of tomorrow, the world of the coming century is your world, dear friends. And your thoughts and deeds today determine largely what it will be like.

Here, in the native land of the great Lenin, you can see for yourselves how deeply our youth is dedicated to the lofty ideals of humanism, peace and socialism.

I believe that all of us will agree that at the present time mankind has no more important, vital task than to safeguard and strengthen peace. Our concern for tomorrow and remembrance of the things past oblige us to do so.

Your forum is held in the year of the fortieth anniversary of the defeat of Hitlerite fascism and Japanese militarism, the end of the Second World War, the most bloody and bitter war. It left so much suffering and sorrow that they tell on the life of already several generations and demand that we prevent such a disaster from recurring.

The peoples shall not forget that fourty years ago the world shook from the first atomic blast. The echo of that blast appeals to the conscience and reason of every upright man. And everyone should ask himself what he has done to prevent nuclear weapons from being put to use ever again, either on earth or in space, to eliminate those weapons completely and for good. To ask himself and to do what he can for our common home—the planet earth.

Unfortunately—and you are aware of this—reactionary forces, to which wars and the arms race bring huge profits, are still actively at work. These forces would like to turn back the course of history, to retain their power and privileges, to dictate their will to peoples.

As for the Soviet Union, I would like to say yet another time with all certainty that a world without wars and weapons, a world of good-neighborliness and cooperation in good faith, a world of friendship among nations are the ideals of socialism, the goals of our policy.

We set ourselves the task of doing away with the arms race; not in word, but in deed we come out for the most radical solution of the problem of nuclear weapons: their complete banning and elimination.

We come out for the strength and energy of people, human genius, to be channeled not to the creation of ever-new means of destruction, but to the elimination of hunger, poverty, diseases, to working for prosperity and peaceful development. We oppose the policy of threats and violence, the trampling of human rights and, in the first place, such sacred rights as the right to life, the right to work. We oppose the turning of newly free and developing countries into a source of the enrichment of monopolies and their utilization as sites for military bases and springboards of aggression.

We say openly and clearly: The Soviet Union sides with those who fight for freedom, national independence, and social justice.

Dear friends,

Soviet people are engaged in peaceful, creative labor. We have achieved much and built much. However, even more remains to be done. There are many spheres in which Soviet young people can apply their skill and knowledge. We appreciate grately their contribution to the present-day work of the Soviet people. And we are absolutely sure that your youth will further measure up to its noble predestination—to continue the building of a new society.

You, participants in the festival, young men and women, personify the spring of mankind, progress and aspirations of your peoples.

So let us tirelessly work for the present and the future of mankind without wars, violence and oppression!

Let the 12th World Fesitval of Youth and Students become a convincing demonstration of solidarity, the allegiance to peace and friendship between nations!

I wish you success and happiness!

July 27, 1985

26

STATEMENT
ON THE
ARMS RACE

T HE CONTINUING nuclear-armaments race is fraught with an immense threat to the future of world civilization. It is leading to higher tensions in the international arena and a greater war danger, diverting enormous intellectual and material resources away from constructive purposes.

From the very beginning of the nuclear age, the Soviet Union has fought consistently and vigorously to end the accumulation of nuclear weapons, to curb military rivalry, to strengthen trust and peaceful cooperation among nations. The whole of the activity of the Soviet Union conducted on a vast scale within the United Nations framework and at multilateral and bilateral talks on the limitation and reduction of armaments is projected toward this goal. The Soviet Union is not seeking military superiority — it favors maintaining the balance of military forces at the lowest possible level.

It is our conviction that ending all tests of nuclear weapons would be a major contribution to the strengthening of strategic stability and peace on earth. It is no secret that new, ever-more perilous kinds and types of weapons of mass annihilation are developed and perfected in the course of such tests.

In the interest of creating favorable conditions for an international treaty on a complete and universal ban on nuclear-weapons tests, the Soviet Union has proposed repeatedly that the nuclear states agree to a moratorium on all nuclear blasts, starting from an agreed date. Regrettably, it has not yet been possible to take this important step.

Seeking to facilitate the termination of the dangerous competition in building up nuclear arsenals, and wishing to set a good example, the Soviet Union has decided to stop unilaterally any nuclear explosions, starting from August 6 this year. We call on the government of the United States to stop its nuclear explosions, starting from this date which is observed worldwide as the day of the Hiroshima tragedy. Our moratorium shall be operative until January 1, 1986. It will remain in effect, however, as long as the

United States, on its part, refrains from conducting nuclear explosions.

Undoubtedly, a mutual moratorium by the Soviet Union and the United States on all nuclear blasts would be a good example for other states possessing nuclear weapons.

The Soviet Union expects the United States to give a positive response to this initiative and to stop its nuclear explosions.

This move would be in accordance with the aspirations and hopes of all nations.

July 29, 1985

27

REPLY
TO A MESSAGE FROM
THE JAPANESE COUNCIL OF
ORGANIZATIONS OF VICTIMS
OF ATOMIC BOMBINGS

Dear Madam Ito,

I was very moved by your letter.

I sympathize deeply with the grief and terrible sufferings experienced by the victims of the barbarous American atomic bombings of Hiroshima and Nagasaki.

I share fully your fervent wish that the tragedy of Hiroshima and Nagasaki never be repeated anywhere in the world, that there be no new victims of nuclear arms on our planet.

The Soviet Union has been pressing for the liquidation of nuclear arms since their first appearance. As far back as 1946, our country proposed that an international convention be concluded prohibiting atomic arms, but this proposal was blocked by the United States. And today, as well, we encounter a lack of readiness on the part of the West to agree to the complete prohibition and liquidation of nuclear arms, and are thus faced with the need to search for possible interim solutions to this paramount problem.

Today, too, the Soviet Union is working actively to eliminate nuclear weapons. We are prepared to begin nuclear disarmament at any time, given agreement with the other nuclear powers. The Soviet Union is holding talks with the United States in Geneva in order to prevent an arms race in outer space, to terminate it on earth, and to begin drastic cuts in nuclear armaments which will result in their total elimination. The position taken by the American side at these talks, however, is blocking the attainment of accord.

The Soviet Union will not initiate nuclear war; it has pledged not to be the first to use nuclear weapons. If all nuclear powers took the same step, favorable conditions would be created for an international treaty banning the use of nuclear weapons.

Our new peace initiative—the decision to unilaterally refrain from all nuclear explosions beginning August 6 of this year, the anniversary of the Hiroshima tragedy—is directed at ending the dangerous rivalry in building up nuclear arsenals. Our moratorium will be operative until January 1, 1986, but will remain in effect as long as the United States, in its turn, refrains from conducting nuclear blasts.

The unqualified approval and broad support with which this initiative has been met by world public opinion confirms that it is in accordance with the aspirations and hopes of all peoples. Now it is the turn of the United States and other countries with nuclear weapons to stop their nuclear explosions. This would be not only a tribute to the memory of the victims of the atomic bombings of Hiroshima and Nagasaki, but also a real contribution to the consolidation of strategic stability and peace on earth. In this way favorable conditions would be created for concluding an international treaty on the complete and universal banning of nuclear-weapons tests.

Our country sympathizes with the striving of many countries to create nuclear-free zones in various parts of the globe. For example, we are for such zones being set up in Northern Europe, the Balkans, Southeast Asia and Africa. The efforts of South Pacific states aimed at creating a nuclear-free zone in their region are praiseworthy.

On the eve of the fortieth anniversary of the atomic bombings of Hiroshima and Nagasaki, it is particularly urgent that no one contravene the nonnuclear status of Japan enshrined in the "three nonnuclear principles" which, as we understand, are an expression of the will of the Japanese people. The Soviet Union honors these principles. It is vital that others do as well — and not just in word, but in deed.

Yet we cannot ignore the growing attempts to turn Japan into a U.S. nuclear base, increase its military role both within the system of alliance with the United States and in the present world in general. Such attempts are fraught with the aggravation of tension in the Far East and in the Asian-Pacific region. Apparently, not everyone has yet drawn the proper conclusions from the lessons of the Second World War, from the atomic bombings of Hiroshima and Nagasaki.

The Soviet people, who lost over 20 million lives during the Second World War, are fully resolved to prevent nuclear catastrophe. The tragedy of Hiroshima and Nagasaki is well known in our country. The Soviet people stand in solidarity with the antiwar, antinuclear movement in Japan and in other countries, which favors complete and ultimate elimination of the nuclear threat all over the world. This movement will be all the stronger, the more representative it is and the more united are its ranks.

I wish the Japanese Council of Organizations of Victims of Atomic Bombings and all its members every success in the struggle to prevent nuclear war, to prohibit and eliminate nuclear weapons.

Yours respectfully,
Mikhail Gorbachev

August 5, 1985

REPLIES
TO QUESTIONS
PUT BY TASS

QUESTION: How would you eval-
uate the reaction of the world to the new Soviet initiative: the
introduction of a moratorium on nuclear explosions?

Answer: If one is to speak of the sentiments of the public at
large, there would appear to be every reason to say that the new
initiative of the Soviet Union, which has discontinued all nuclear
explosions unilaterally and called upon the United States to follow
suit, has been received with approval in the world. In many countries, including the United States, prominent statesmen, political
and public figures have been declaring support for the idea of a
moratorium on nuclear weapons tests and urging other nuclear
powers to follow the Soviet Union's example. We have proposed a
concrete, tangible measure. People see in it a hope for slowing
down and then halting the nuclear arms race.

I know that our initiative is not to everyone's liking. Those in
the West who have inked their policy with further escalation of the
arms race and who derive considerable profits from it do not want
an end to nuclear tests. They oppose the moratorium because they
do not want the nuclear-arms production lines to come to a stand-
still. They cling to unattainable illusions of gaining military superiority one way or another. At the same time they are spreading
falsehoods about the Soviet Union's policies, including those in
connection with the moratorium on nuclear explosions that we have
announced.

The moratorium was an honest and open move on our part. We
introduced steps to stop the buildup and further improvement of
nuclear arms. We had no intention at all of placing the U.S.
leadership in a difficult position. The President of the United States
was notified in advance of our move by a letter in which we
suggested that the American side take the same step. We would like
the U.S. leadership to respond positively to this call of ours.
Unfortunately, public pronouncements by officials in Washington

---

The interview was published in *Pravda* on August 14, 1985.

on the moratorium issue create the impression that there they are now preoccupied mostly with finding the most adroit way of evading such a response. I shall not be mistaken if I say that the world expects a different attitude.

Question: President Reagan said the other day that the United States could not afford a moratorium on nuclear tests because it has to complete its nuclear programs. At the same time, he asserted that the Soviet Union had completed an intensive series of nuclear explosions and could afford a respite. Is that so?

Answer: The decision to discontinue nuclear explosions unilaterally was made by the Soviet leadership after thorough study from every angle. It was not all that easy to take such a step. To introduce a unilateral moratorium, we had to interrupt the test program and leave it unfinished.

In the current year before the moratorium, nearly the same number of nuclear explosions were carried out in the Soviet Union as in the United States. But if one speaks of all the nuclear tests that have been carried out to date, their number is much greater in the United States than in the Soviet Union. And the White House knows it.

But in taking the decision on a unilateral moratorium, the Soviet Union was guided not by arithmetic, but by political considerations of principle, by a desire to help end the nuclear arms race and to urge the United States and the other countries possessing nuclear weapons to take such a step. Our goal is complete and general termination of nuclear weapons tests, and not some respite between explosions.

The opinion has been voiced that the introduction of a moratorium on nuclear explosions is allegedly not in the interests of the United States. But a moratorium is an important step toward ending further perfection of lethal nuclear weapons. Besides, the longer the period without tests, the more rapid will be the process of "aging" of the stockpiled weapons. And, finally, a moratorium creates more favorable conditions for agreement on the termination of nuclear tests and for making headway toward scrapping nuclear weapons altogether.

The question arises: What does not accord with the interests of the United States, of the American people? This course does not suit those who count on power politics, who devise plans to create ever-new types of nuclear weapons on earth and who have set themselves the aim of launching an arms race in outer space. But what has this to do with the genuine interests of strengthening peace and international security, a desire which has been professed repeatedly in Washington?

Attempts are being made to explain the unwillingness to end nuclear tests by the assertion that the United States "lags behind" in nuclear arms. But this is merely a pretext. At one time there was talk about a "lag" in bombers, and later on it was missiles. However, each time that was a deliberate deception which was subsequently admitted in Washington. In other words, talk about a "lag" begins whenever there is a striving to achieve military superiority and when there is no real desire to settle arms-limitation issues. It is precisely on these matters that decisions should be taken by the political leadership—and not on the basis of diverse myths about the "Soviet threat," but proceeding from the actual situation and the genuine security interests of one's country and the interests of international security.

Question: How do you visualize the issue of verification in the context of the proposal to end nuclear explosions?

Answer: The scientific and technical possibilities existing in this country, the United States and other countries give sufficient grounds for confidence that a nuclear explosion—even of a low yield—will be detected and will become known. Those who say the contrary know that it is not so.

Of course, unilateral steps to end nuclear explosions cannot resolve altogether the problem of a complete and general cessation of nuclear weapons tests. For this problem to be solved once and for all, an international agreement is needed. Apart from the relevant commitments, it would also contain an appropriate system of verification measures—both national and international. In short, we are for verification of the ending of nuclear explosions, but we are against cessation of tests being substituted by their continuation in the presence of observers.

It will be recalled that the problem of the complete and general termination of nuclear weapons tests is by no means new. Several year ago it was examined in detail in tripartite talks between the Soviet Union, the United States and Great Britain. At that time, verification was also discussed in great detail. In many respects, the sides came close to mutual understanding. But the United States broke off the talks because the limitations being worked out hindered the Pentagon's plans.

We have proposed repeatedly to the United States that the talks be resumed. And today, as well, we are calling on it to do this: to achieve complete cessation of nuclear-weapons tests. The holding of such talks and the achievement of results at them would be much easier in conditions when the Soviet Union and the United States would not be conducting nuclear tests. However, the United States does not want to return to the negotiating table. And this means that the United States does not want either an end to nuclear tests or a reliable system of verification. That is the only conclusion that can be made.

It is sometimes said that the question of ending nuclear-weapons tests should be considered at the Geneva Conference on Disarmament. Very well, we are prepared to discuss it there, too. But, in Geneva, the United States and other Western countries have been sabotaging the conduct of such talks for a long time. Therefore, the point is not where to consider the cessation of nuclear-weapons tests. What is important is to consider this problem seriously and without delay, with a view to the forthcoming Soviet-American meeting.

Question: Is it possible, nonetheless, in your opinion, to expect a positive solution to the question of nuclear tests?

Answer: I think it is. Although the present attitude of the United States to our proposal does not inspire optimism, one would not like to lose hope. The reason is this: Too great a responsibility rests on the Soviet Union and the United States for them to evade the solution of major security matters.

What we suggest is a real possibility to stop the further buildup of nuclear arsenals and to tackle in earnest the task of reducing and ultimately eliminating them.

29

A MESSAGE
OF GREETINGS TO THE
PARTICIPANTS IN THE
CONFERENCE
REVIEWING THE
TREATY ON THE
NON-PROLIFERATION OF
NUCLEAR WEAPONS

I GREET THE representatives of the states, participants to the Treaty on the Non-Proliferation of Nuclear Weapons, who have gathered in Geneva at a conference to review how that most important international agreement has worked.

The Non-Proliferation Treaty, drawn up by the collective efforts of many states, has demonstrated in practice its viability. Not a single state has acquired nuclear weapons since the treaty's conclusion. It is the broadest arms-control accord in terms of the number of parties adhering to it. An international order on nonproliferation has emerged on its oasis and become an effective instrument for peace.

Another important result of the Non-Proliferation Treaty is that it has provided favorable conditions for broad international cooperation in the use of atomic energy for peaceful purposes, which, in its turn, is so necessary for the solution of the problem of supplying energy to mankind and other major economic problems of concern to all peoples. The International Atomic Energy Agency has done a good service in the practical accomplishment of these tasks.

The Soviet Union stands resolutely for further expansion and development of such cooperation. It is important that atomic energy should really become an asset of the whole of mankind and serve only the purposes of peace and construction.

In keeping with its commitments under the treaty, the Soviet Union has been doing and will continue to do everything within its power not only to prevent the proliferation of nuclear weapons, but to halt and reverse the nuclear arms race.

The Soviet Union has more than once taken unilateral steps, setting examples for others and thus contributing to the drafting of agreements on limiting and halting the nuclear arms race. The Soviet Union has assumed a commitment not to be the first to use nuclear weapons. If those nuclear powers that have not yet done so had followed suit, it would have been equivalent, on the whole, to a general ban on the use of nuclear weapons.

Fresh evidence of our desire to ease the way to winding down the nuclear arms race is the proclamation by the Soviet Union of a moratorium on all nuclear explosions. It is beyond doubt that a mutual Soviet-American moratorium on nuclear explosions could provide favorable conditions for an international treaty on the complete and universal prohibition of nuclear weapons tests and contribute to a fuller implementation of the provisions of the Treaty on the Non-Proliferation of Nuclear Weapons.

The problem of curbing the nuclear arms race in the nuclear and space age is inseparable from the task of preventing the militarization of outer space. If outer space is put to the service of war, the nuclear threat will be dramatically escalated. But if outer space is kept peaceful and kept out of the sphere of military rivalry, an impulse could be given to the solution of the entire range of questions regarding the limitation and reduction of nuclear-arms arsenals. Simultaneously, broad possibilities would be opened for comprehensive international cooperation in various fields of human activity, both on earth and in outer space. It is for these reasons that at the 40th UN General Assembly the Soviet Union introduces for discussion definite proposals on international cooperation in the peaceful exploration of outer space under conditions of its nonmilitarization.

In short, we stand for energetic work in curbing the arms race in every area. Measures to prevent the spread of nuclear weapons clearly continue to play an important role.

I wish the participants in the conference success in their efforts to further strengthen the Treaty on the Non-Proliferation of Nuclear Weapons.

Mikhail Gorbachev
August 27, 1985

30

LETTER
TO
MRS. JANE SMITH

Dear Mrs. Jane Smith,

Please accept my deep condolences on the tragic death of your daughter Samantha and husband Arthur.

Everyone in the Soviet Union who knew Samantha Smith will remember forever the image of the American girl who, like millions of Soviet young men and women, dreamed of peace and friendship between the peoples of the United States and the Soviet Union.

Respectfully,

Mikhail Gorbachev
August 28, 1985

31

SPEECH AT A DINNER
IN HONOR OF
JAMBYN BATMÖNKH

DEAR Comrade Batmönkh,
Dear Comrades,
Our working meeting is drawing to a close. I think there is every reason to be satisfied with its results. It is yet another indication of the complete mutual understanding and confidence between the leadership of the Communist Party of the Soviet Union (CPSU) and the Mongolian People's Revolutionary Party (MPRP).

In the discussion we had, we told each other, in a comradely manner, about the efforts and plans of our fraternal parties and countries. The Soviet Communists and all Soviet people are glad that the working people of Mongolia, under the MPRP's leadership, are successfully carrying out the resolutions of the 18th Party Congress and of the subsequent plenary meetings of its Central Committee and are working hard to accelerate their country's social and economic progress. With all our hearts, we wish our Mongolian friends further success in the confident advancement toward new frontiers in the building of socialism.

In the course of our meeting, we have reviewed Soviet-Mongolian relations thoroughly. It is well known that the friendship and alliance of our parties, countries and peoples have deep historical roots and a sound internationalist foundation. Close cooperation, which the great Lenin and the leader of the Mongolian Revolution, Sühe Baator, called on us to maintain, has been invariably on the rise. It embraces literally every area of life today. One distinguishing feature of Soviet-Mongolian relations at the present stage is that they involve the widest sections of the working people, who are united by an understanding of the common historical destinies of our peoples and by a mutual feeling of sympathy and respect.

While paying respect to what has been achieved, we are now concentrating our efforts on enhancing the effectiveness of Soviet-Mongolian cooperation in political, economic, social, cultural and other fields.

An important step forward has been taken today with the signing of the Long-Term Program for the Promotion of Economic,

Scientific, and Technological Cooperation Between the Soviet Union and Mongolia for the period ending in the year 2000. It is a document of great political importance. Its implementation will make it possible to make fuller use of the potentialities and reserves of the Soviet-Mongolian relationship, to pool our efforts and experience, our resources and knowledge more rationally for building up the economic potential and advancing the well-being of the working people. And that responds not only to the basic interests of the peoples of our two countries, but also to the common objectives of strengthening the positions of the socialist community.

Today's meeting proves once again that we are at one with our Mongolian friends in the assessment of the present international situation. Through the fault of imperialism, it remains tense and demands the vigilance of all those concerned with the present and the future of humanity.

What I said applies in full measure to the Asian-Pacific region, the developments in which are of close concern both to the Soviet Union and to Mongolia. The militaristic activity of imperialist states there is acquiring growing dimensions. At present, there are hundreds of American military installations in the Far East, where the United States has the second largest concentration of its overseas armed forces.

Japan, whose government has been voicing its readiness to cooperate in the American "Star Wars" program, is hitching itself up increasingly to the U.S. war chariot. This course of events means aggravating instability in the region, enlarging the old hotbeds of military-political tension and breeding more conflict situations.

The need to oppose the intrigues of imperialism and reaction in Asia should be emphasized now, when the peoples in the Asian-Pacific region, together with progressives all over the world, are marking the fortieth anniversary of the victory over Japanese militarism. The growing activities of the antiwar forces in that region are a convincing indicator of the mounting concern felt by public opinion in the Asian countries for the destiny of peace.

The Soviet Union, Mongolia and other socialist countries have recently put forward a series of specific initiatives aimed at normalizing the situation in Asia and the Pacific area. The decision taken by the Soviet government to unilaterally cease all nuclear explosions as of August 6, 1985, meets the vital security interests of all peoples in the world. This decision is of particular significance for the Asian-Pacific region: It was precisely here that both American atomic bombs were dropped.

Recently this country has come forward with a proposal that a general and comprehensive approach be elaborated to deal with security problems in Asia. In substance, it proposes that all Asian countries should combine their efforts, regardless of their social system, to ensure peace and stability. This proposal stems from the fundamental principles of the Leninist foreign policy followed by the CPSU, which was the first in history to proclaim the idea of peaceful coexistence. This proposal takes into account the entire totality of experience accumulated in various parts of the world in the effort to ease tensions and to achieve détente.

We realize, of course, that there are difficulties – and considerable ones – in the way of consolidating peace in the Asian-Pacific region. They are due to disagreements between states of the region and to their different approaches to existing problems. But the Asian peoples are linked by common vital interests and tackle largely similar tasks engendered by the past and facing them as they look to the future, and this is more important. It is this which dictates the necessity of cooperation and good-neighborly relations built on a broad-based agreement on security that would conform to the interests of each and every country in the region.

As we see it, such an agreement could incorporate the five principles of peaceful coexistence *(pancha shila)* formulated previously by Asian countries, the ten principles of Bandung, a number of the initiatives of the Soviet Union, the Mongolian People's Republic, the Democratic People's Republic of Korea, the Indochina countries, India and other states of the region on the problems of security in Asia, on transforming the Indian Ocean into a zone of peace and other important issues.

Asian security would no doubt be strengthened if the nuclear powers ceased all nuclear weapons tests everywhere, including Asia and the Pacific and Indian oceans, and if the states of the region refused to take part in the plans to militarize space.

Needless to say, these provisions can be developed and supplemented by collective efforts. Noteworthy, for example, are proposals on not using force, respect for the sovereignty and territorial integrity of all countries in the region, on the implementation of confidence-building measures in the military-political field, and some other proposals.

The working out and putting into effect of an agreement on Asian security are obviously long-term tasks. Their implementation needs a stage-by-stage approach—from the simple to the more complex. The Soviet Union will treat with understanding any proposals prompted by genuine concern for peace and security in Asia.

Dear Mongolian friends,

We are meeting in a momentous period when preparations have begun in our countries for party congresses. These preparations are keynoted by the adherence of the working people of the Soviet Union and Mongolia to the ideas of Marxism-Leninism and socialist internationalism. These ideas, which have united us forever, are inspiring us to tireless work in the name of socialism and peace.

Allow me to wish you, dear Comrade Batmönkh, the leadership of the Mongolian People's Revolutionary Party and the entire fraternal Mongolian people, new, great success in this work, happiness and prosperity.

MEETING WITH
U.S. SENATORS

MIKHAIL Gorbachev, General Secretary of the CPSU Central Committee, a Member of the Presidium of the Supreme Soviet of the Soviet Union, received U.S. Senate Democratic leader Robert Byrd, President Pro Tempore of the Senate Strom Thurmond and Senators Claiborne Pell, Sam Nunn, Dennis DeConcini, Paul Sarbanes, John Warner and George Mitchell in the Kremlin on September 3. The senators were invited to the Soviet Union by the Parlimentary Group of the Soviet Union.

During the meeting, Mikhail Gorbachev appraised the present state of Soviet-American relations and the international situation as a whole.

The Soviet Union, he said, stands sincerely for returning Soviet-American relations to the channel of normal, correct and mutually advantageous cooperation, for getting a constructive dialogue going between our countries, for establishing at least a minimum of mutual trust and respect for each other's legitimate interests.

He pointed out that the main task today is to put an end to the arms race, to ensure a turn toward peaceful development and mutually advantageous cooperation. The decisive factor in Soviet-American relations is the state of affairs in the sphere of security. That is why the search for agreements on really major, central problems should be carried on in this sphere. Primarily, these are the problems concerning space and nuclear arms that are being discussed at the Geneva negotiations, as well as measures of military détente and the building up of trust in the broadest sense.

The Soviet people's intensive creative life, the far-reaching plans of our peaceful constructive effort all determine the peaceable character of the Soviet Union's foreign policy.

He drew the U.S. Senators' attention to the important peace initiatives that the Soviet Union has put forward recently, including the moratorium imposed by the Soviet side on nuclear explosions and the appeal to the United States to follow suit, as well as the proposal made by the Soviet Union at the United Nations on international cooperation in the peaceful exploration of outer space in conditions of its nonmilitarization. The implementation of these proposals would contribute to a radical resolution of the long-standing problems of space and nuclear armaments, strengthen mutual trust and military détente, and be a good incentive for practical advancement toward the ultimate goal: the elimination of all nuclear weapons everywhere, the strengthening of international security and universal peace.

These initiatives have met with worldwide approval. Many people see in them real hope for ending, at last, the nuclear-arms race, for keeping outer space free from weapons. Prominent scientists and public figures, among them Americans, call for a response to these courageous Soviet initiatives. Such voices can also be heard in the U.S. Congress, which could certainly make a big contribution to the resolution of the problems existing between our two countries.

The Soviet Union and the United States, Mikhail Gorbachev pointed out, are the greatest military powers and will, to all appearances, remain such. Neither of the sides will resign itself to the other's gaining a lasting or decisive superiority. One cannot help drawing a conclusion from this fact: No test of strength should be held, matters should not be brought to a dangerous confrontation.

The positions of our two countries on a number of issues do not coincide, which is predetermined by the major differences between our two systems. But however deep these differences may be, they should not and cannot obstruct the main goal: our responsibility for averting the nuclear threat, for preserving peace.

Mikhail Gorbachev noted the importance of developing contacts between the USSR Supreme Soviet and the U.S. Congress, stressing that these contacts should serve the interests of peace and help normalize relations between the two countries.

Touching upon the Soviet-American summit, which the sides have agreed upon, Mikhail Gorbachev emphasized that the Soviet side was going to that meeting with sincere goodwill and with a desire to do everything possible to strengthen peace. It is necessary that the meeting should satisfy not only the peoples of our countries, but the peoples of the whole world. If the American side also displays goodwill, the meeting can produce positive results.

Senator Robert Byrd and the other U.S. Senators expressed their thanks for a clear presentation of the Soviet position and noted the usefulness of the talk with Mikhail Gorbachev and the need for extending dialogue, improving the atmosphere in relations between the two countries, and developing mutually beneficial contacts in different fields. They called for the success of the forthcoming summit. At the same time, the American side repeated the arguments which, in large measure, amount to a justification of the U.S. Administration's course in whipping up the arms race, even in space.

Mikhail Gorbachev emphasized, in this context, the need for a responsible and serious approach by statesmen, including parliamentarians, to the questions of vital importance for the peoples of the two countries and of the whole world.

September 3, 1985

33

TO THE PARTICIPANTS IN THE INTERNATIONAL CONFERENCE MARKING FORTY YEARS SINCE THE VICTORY OVER JAPANESE MILITARISM

I SEND CORDIAL greetings to the participants in the international conference, who have gathered in the Soviet Union's major Far Eastern center, the city of Khabarovsk, to exchange views on outstanding questions of ensuring peace and security in the Asian and Pacific countries.

Your meeting has been timed to coincide with an important anniversary, forty years since the defeat of Japanese militarism and the victorious ending of the Second World War. The great victory, won at the cost of immense sacrifices, delivered many Asian and Pacific peoples from hated foreign occupation and created preconditions for a strong upsurge of the anticolonial struggle and for winning political independence and state sovereignty. It also delivered the Japanese people from the tyranny of the military-fascist clique and opened before them the possibility to follow a peaceful road of development.

The five principles of peaceful coexistence *(pancha shila)* that won recognition all over the world as a norm for relations between states with different social systems were formulated and proclaimed on the ancient soil of Asia and on the basis of the tragic experience of the past war. It was also there that the spirit of Bandung emerged, which gave rise to the movement of Afro-Asian solidarity and to the nonaligned movement, which has now become an important factor in world politics.

Nowadays, when the threat of a world nuclear-missile catastrophe looms over the earth, there is no more important and urgent a task than that of safeguarding world peace. The militarist forces of imperialism are pursuing a policy of aggression in that vast region of the world, hatching plans to turn it into a scene of military-political confrontation with socialist and many nonaligned countries, pressing for the remilitarization of Japan and for the establishment of an aggressive Washington—Tokyo—Seoul grouping.

Dangerous plans and preparations for aggression are being countered by the policy of peace pursued by the Soviet Union and the other countries of the socialist community, and by the growing commitment of the Asian peoples to the idea of turning Asia into a zone of peace and security, a zone of equal and mutually beneficial international cooperation. This goal is also being pursued by the Soviet Union's unilateral moratorium on all nuclear explosions from August 6, the anniversary of the barbarous atomic bombing of Hiroshima by the U.S. Air Force.

The Soviet Union has put forward many concrete proposals for easing the situation in Asia and for asserting on the continent the spirit of peaceful coexistence, good-neighborliness, respect for sovereignty and noninterference in the internal affairs of other states.

Our country greatly appreciates and supports the counstructive peace initiatives of other Asian countries bearing on various aspects of Asian security as a whole or aimed to improve the situation in individual regions of the continent. We express the hope that the Asian states will pool their efforts to work out jointly a common, comprehensive approach to the problem of security in the whole of Asia and in the adjacent areas of the Pacific and Indian oceans.

I believe that the public and political forces and organizations in the Asian and Pacific countries, together with all the progressive forces of the world, will be even more vigorous in their struggle for ending the arms race, removing the threat of world nuclear war, eliminating nuclear weapons and improving the international situation.

I wish your conference success in its work.

Mikhail Gorbachev
September 5, 1985

34

LETTER TO THE INDIAN INSTITUTE FOR INSTITUTE FOR NONALIGNED STUDIES

I SINCERELY thank the leaders of the Indian Institute for Nonaligned Studies for the warm, friendly message, for the ardent expression of support for the Soviet Union's peaceable foreign-policy initiatives, which are directed at lessening international tensions and eliminating the threat of nuclear war.

I would like to note that in the interests of creating favorable conditions for concluding an international treaty on a complete and general ban of nuclear weapons tests, the Soviet Union has proposed repeatedly that the countries possessing nuclear weapons agree on a moratorium on all nuclear blasts. Unfortunately, this goal has not been achieved so far. Our latest initiative on that issue is not to everybody's liking in the West. The U.S. administration apparently has no wish to follow the example of the Soviet Union, which has halted nuclear blasts unilaterally until the end of the year. Washington is continuing its policy of stepping up the arms race and is continuing nuclear tests. Meanwhile, if the United States acceded to our initiative, it would be possible to extend the moratorium introduced by us and substantially improve the chances of solving on the whole, the problem of ending nuclear tests.

Implementation of practical measures in the field of disarmament would make it possible to release enormous funds and place them at the service of mankind's peaceful development, including the solution of such acute problems as poverty, hunger, disease, and illiteracy, which have not yet been eradicated in many countries that were the objects of colonial exploitation and plunder in the not-so-distant past.

The Soviet people highly appreciate India's contribution to the struggle for peace and the security of nations. The voice of the 700 million peace-loving Indian people is heeded not only in Asia, but also far beyond its borders. Being the recognized leader of the nonaligned movement, India does a great deal to strengthen and develop it.

We are deeply convinced that the dynamically developing friendship and cooperation between the Soviet Union and India and their commitment to peace are important factors in preventing the threat of thermonuclear war and in preserving life on earth.

Mikhail Gorbachev
September 6, 1985

The Indian Institute for Nonaligned Studies sent a letter to Mikhail Gorbachev, ardently welcoming the Soviet Union's decision to unilaterally halt all nuclear blasts as a new major peaceful initiative of the Soviet Union aimed at lessening tensions and creating a favorable climate for international cooperation and mutual understanding in strengthening peace throughout the world.

The Indian Institute for Nonaligned Studies says that it is convinced that the Soviet Union's initiative will be approved and supported by all peace-loving nations which will unite their efforts to achieve complete nuclear disarmament.

35

MESSAGE OF GREETINGS
TO THE GENERAL COUNCIL
OF THE
WORLD FEDERATION
OF TRADE UNIONS

I cordially greet the participants in the session of the General Council of the World Federation of Trade Unions being held on the eve of the fortieth anniversary of the WFTU. Born in an atmosphere of the upsurge in the world working-class movement evoked by the route of Hitler nazism and the victorious end to the second World War, the Federation has traversed a long and glorious path, making an important contribution to the cause of international consolidation of the working people.

Today the WFTU is the biggest international confederation of working people. Its ranks have been cooperating on a class basis with trade unions working in countries with various social systems.

The organizations incorporated in the WFTU uphold the rights of the working people, consistently and resolutely opposing imperialism, neocolonialism and racism, and the predatory policy of international monopolies. They are fighting for peace, democracy, freedom, and social progress. In the socialist countries, they are playing a growing role in sociopolitical life. They are involved actively in building and developing a new society, and carrying out large-scale and wide-ranging work in the interests of the working people.

The continuing deterioration in the international situation increases the alarm of the peoples for the future of peace. The arms race unleashed by the most aggressive imperialist circles and the military-industrial complex not only effects the position of working people adversely, but calls into question mankind's very future.

Another path is required by the working people: one of returning to détente and applying the manpower and material resources absorbed by the arms race to resolve acute socioeconomic problems like eliminating mass unemployment, economic backwardness, hunger, and illiteracy, and establishing a new international economic order. The success of the drive for these goals depends in large measure on the trade unions, on the international working class as a whole.

The Soviet Union resolutely advocates such a development.

Our goal is radical improvement in the international situation, elimination of the military threat, an end to the arms race on earth, and the forestalling of them in space and the reduction in deadly nuclear arsenals to the extent of total elimination.

I am confident that the Soviet trade unions, which took part in establishing and developing the World Federation of Trade Unions, will continue working actively in that representative international organization, and will contribute to enhancing the effectiveness of its activities, firmly establishing in the world trade union movement the ideas of cohesion of action. They will continue to adhere firmly to positions of proletarian internationalism and to support the just struggle of their class brothers abroad. Working people's solidarity is the mighty power source of the trade union movement.

I wish the World Federation of Trade Unions fresh success as it acts for the good of the working people and campaigns for social progress, for peace and friendship among nations.

Mikhail Gorbachev
October 1, 1985

36

ADDRESS ON FRENCH TELEVISION

O<small>N</small> September 30, Mikhail Gorbachev received Yves Mourousi, Alain d'Anvers and Dominique Bromberge, journalists of the French television company TF-1, on the occasion of his upcoming official visit to France.

Below is the text of Mikhail Gorbachev's address to French television viewers and his replies to the questions the TF-1 representatives sent him.

Good evening, ladies and gentlemen,

Good evening, dear friends,

I am glad to have an opportunity to meet French television viewers on the eve of my visit to your country. I must say that I am looking forward with much interest to this new meeting with France, her people, political leaders, and public figures.

I share the opinion of the President of the French Republic that the forthcoming meeting is of a special nature for many reasons. We will certainly judge it by its results, but now I will say that we are preparing for the meeting with a sense of high responsibility, and, on our part, will do our utmost for it to be fruitful.

As far as bilateral relations are concerned, we are convinced that development of Soviet-French cooperation accords with the vital interests of both peoples. The best proof of that is historical experience. When Russia and France and the Soviet Union and France have cooperated, this has served the best interests of both of them, just as of the whole of Europe and of the whole world, for that matter. And, on the contrary, alienation and enmity were detrimental to our national interests and affected the international atmosphere adversely.

One cannot strike out of history the fact that Soviet people and Frenchmen were brothers-in-arms in the struggle against fascism. We would betray the memory of the fallen in that sacred struggle if we were to forget how the French pilots of the Normandy-Neman Regiment fought heroically against the fascists in Soviet skies, and how the Soviet partisans fought in the ranks of the Maquis on

French soil.

Twenty million Soviet people died in that terrible war, and they died for our and your freedom. Frenchmen, too, sacrificed their lives for your and our freedom. More than twenty thousand Soviet antifascist fighters are buried in France. I know that their memory is revered in your country. The Soviet people are grateful to you for your feelings of respect.

But it is not only that joint victory that brings the Soviet and French peoples close together. Our cooperation in many fields — in economics and trade, literature and the arts — has deep roots that go down through the ages. All this is indicative of good fundamentals, good traditions, and deep roots to our relations. Development and strengthening thereof — and I say this with great confidence — serves our common interests. It is most important not only to continue, but also to deepen the dialogue, accord, and cooperation between the Soviet Union and France.

On the whole, as it seems to us, our relations are shaping up quite well. The volume of trade has grown fourfold in ten years. We are gratified by that. And I believe this also serves the best interests of France. Yet our economic relations could be more active and diversified. Such is our belief. The same goes for cooperation in science and technology, where an impressive symbol was the joint flight of Soviet and French cosmonauts. The exchanges in the field of culture and education, tourism, and public contacts are fruitful.

I hope that the forthcoming Soviet-French meeting will give a fresh impetus to the development of political, trade, economic, scientific, technical, cultural and other relations between the Soviet Union and France. But we view this meeting as a major event not only in bilateral relations. Accords and cooperation, as was recorded in the Principles of Soviet-French Relations in 1971, are designed to become a "permanent policy in their relations and a permanent factor in international life."

Another reason for the urgency of my meeting with President Mitterrand is the worsening of the international situation. There is little consolation in what is happening in the world today. At any rate, judging by deeds rather than by words, international tensions are growing. The threat of a nuclear-missile catastrophe is not

declining. We must face this bitter truth. Mountains of arms have
been stockpiled. Yet their production and modernization are being
stepped up. Europe is literally crammed with military bases and
deadly weapons. Today it is an understatement to say that it is a
"powder keg." It is a much more explosive concentration of the latest
means for destruction of human beings. But even this proves not
enough: New gigantic armament programs and most dangerous
strategic concepts are drawn up feverishly and realized, although
Europe is too small and too fragile for policies from the position of
strength, as, for that matter, is the whole of our planet earth.

I am saying all this in the belief that today nobody has the right
to be a passive observer of what is going on. So much distrust and
suspicion have accumulated in the world that it will, perhaps, take
quite a lot of effort and time to dismantle the barriers. But without
that, without an appropriate — what I would call a psychological —
change of attitude and, certainly, without political will it shall be
difficult to change the situation for the better if possible at all. The
destiny of every nation, of every person, whether an ordinary
citizen or a political leader, is being decided in foreign policy now.

To survive and ensure a future for our children and grandchildren, we must curb the forces of madness, the forces of war and
militarism. The flames of war should be extinguished before they
flare up.

Can this be done? We believe that it is possible. We already
have positive experience on which to base our belief — the success of
détente. And that success has preserved its vital force. Consistent
observance of all provisions of the Helsinki Final Act can again
improve the climate in Europe and dispel the clouds that have
gathered over the continent.

Once Voltaire dreamed of the triumph of reason as an indispensable condition for normal human life. This call by the great son of
France is particularly topical today when the crossbow and sword
have been replaced with nuclear weapons. We will have time
enough to find out whose ideology, whose views and laws are more
moral and whose economy is more rational. History will have
enough time for a peaceful competition of ways of life to ensure for
people an opportunity to make a voluntary choice, on their own, to

determine which social system is more to their liking. Yes, we are different, but nothing can be done about that; such is the will of history.

As far as the Soviet Union is concerned, it is doing and will continue to do everything in its power to live in peace with the nations belonging to other systems. Moreover, this is precisely the principle that underlies our approach to the solution of international problems. We are guided by that also in our domestic policy.

Now I will speak briefly about our domestic affairs. About 277 million people live in the Soviet Union today. History has convinced us that the peoples of Russia made the right choice in 1917 by accomplishing the October Revolution, by destroying exploitation, social and national oppression. The Soviet people are proud of their country's achievements, and, in particular, of the fact that for more than fifty years now there has been no unemployment in the country, and the right to work is guaranteed in the Constitution and secured by a system of corresponding social and economic measures. There is no deficit in our national budget.

Our people, just like any other, want to live better and are gratified that in the past two decades real per-capita incomes have doubled, and that staple foodstuff prices have not increased. More than two million apartments are built in the Soviet Union every year. Housing is provided free of charge, and the rent accounts for an average three percent of a family's budget. The health of people and their spiritual development will remain our major concern. Mind you, we have succeeded in achieving a good deal in this field. There are more than six million engineers, 1.5 million scientific workers, and more than a million physicians in our country. A system of free public education and health care has been established and is functioning.

The Soviet Union integrates more than a hundred peoples and nationalities. The assertion of the principle of equality of peoples in all spheres of society's life was one of the principal gains of the Revolution. Of today's fifteen Union Republics and thirty-eight autonomous administrative units, many were backward outlying regions at the time the Revolution took place. Nowadays they not only enjoy equal economic and political rights, but also have created powerful economies of their own and have made great strides in science, culture, and education.

Soviet people see not only their achievements and successes but their weaknesses and shortcomings. You possibly know that all issues are discussed in our society widely, openly, democratically. We consider it important to focus attention precisely on unsolved problems and are striving to accelerate the economic and social development of our country and to improve people's lives. We are sensitive to negligence and irresponsibility. And, of course, we devote primary attention to seeing to it that the norms of social justice, the democratic rights of citizens, and Soviet laws are strictly observed.

All these efforts are approved of by our people – moreover, the people demand of us, their leaders, that we pursue precisely such a policy. I know this from the many thousands of letters I get from people and from personal meetings and contacts with hundreds and hundreds of Soviet people.

To put it in a nutshell, we know the existing problems well. Some questions have been or are being solved, while others require time, resources, and persistent efforts. We have now fundamentally taken up the questions of scientific and technological progress and of improving economic management and management methods. We have the possibilities to solve the new tasks. There are highly qualified cadres, natural resources, and a science-based production potential.

The main point is that our political course is supported widely by all sections of the population. We intend to bring further measures to improve the state of affairs up for discussion by the whole people.

Generally, we will arrive at our party's forthcoming 27th Congress with a definite program of action to perfect Soviet society and with plans for the coming five years and for the period to the end of the century. We will peer with our mind's eye into the third millennium. The prospects that are opening up are vast. Suffice it to say that the amount of work to be done in industry alone in the forthcoming fifteen years is equal to that which we have done over the almost seven decades of Soviet power.

I am saying this not only to acquaint French TV audiences with our everyday work and concerns. It seems important to me that in France and other countries, people should have a clear idea of our priorities. If the main thing for us, the Soviet people, is to develop the economy, social relations, and democracy, then this also determines our interests in the international arena and our foreign policy interests – above all, the interest in peace – and in a stable international situation that would make it possible to concentrate attention and resources on peaceful creative work.

We are resolute opponents of the arms race on earth and of transferring that race into outer space. It is essential to stop this very dangerous process and to begin tackling disarmament without delay.

I want to emphasize that we are not only making statements, but also acting precisely along those lines. We have renounced the first use of nuclear weapons unilaterally, have introduced a moratorium on all nuclear explosions, and have suspended the deployment of medium-range missiles in Europe. We have told the whole world that we shall not be the first to march into outer space with weapons. Our country is ready for other radical solutions as well.

And what does all this mean? Just try to think, without bias, what is being done and said in reply to our initiatives. New nuclear explosions have been carried out, an antisatellite weapon has been tested, and a feverish drumming-up of distrust for our initiatives is under way. It is impossible not to get the impression that some people have been frightened by the very possibility of accords in Geneva, and by the prospect that production of weapons will perhaps have to be curtailed and military appetites moderated. But we shall see what we shall see. Our patience will suffice us. But I want to be frank: All this is very far from a search for ways to improve the international situation.

As you see, quite a number of issues have been building up in the world – disquieting and urgent issues. I intend to discuss them with the President of France most seriously. I trust that our dialogue will be fruitful. I am convinced that the Soviet Union and France have a real possibility to make a tangible contribution to the cause of mutual understanding and cooperation among peoples. It is with this hope that I am going to France.

On behalf of the Soviet people, I wish all TV viewers, all the men and women of France, and all French families happiness, prosperity, and peace.

Best wishes to you all.

D'Anvers: Please accept our thanks for receiving us, Mr. Gorbachev. We are pleased to meet with you here regardless of the views you profess. You are a man of the modern age, a man of your time.

Gorbachev: I hope our meeting will come off in the spirit of mutual understanding and of that traditional friendship that is characteristic of relations between our countries.

Question: You know that not everything will be easy during your visit to France. You are awaited in Paris both with interest and with, I could say, a certain wariness. They want to see what kind of man Mr. Gorbachev is. Also, questions of Soviet-French relations will be discussed regarding both defense policy and human rights. What do you think on this score? Will you now have to revise some positions?

Answer: Why am I going to France on my first foreign visit to the West? I have already tried briefly to answer this question in my address to viewers.

We are aware, of course, that there are likely to be people in France who, perhaps, even frown at the way our relations are shaping up—and those relations are becoming dynamic, making progress and gaining momentum. What I have in mind is both political dialogue and the broadening of economic ties and traditional cultural contacts. We proceed from the assumption that this meets the vital interests of the Soviet people and the vital interests of the French people. This is the decisive thing; the rest are details. Perhaps there are those in France who criticize us. I think that, perhaps, those critics would even like to detract from these good tendencies in the development of Soviet-French relations. But it is not to them that we are looking. I repeat, we are going to France because we think that this meets the vital interests of our countries, the goals of improving the international situation as a whole, and hence the interests of other peoples. Today, more than ever before, we need an active political dialogue to remove the overlayers of past years. We are different, true, and have different political systems and different views of human values, but we also have much in common. First of all, I think, what we have in common is a desire to live in a real world and to find ways to work together and cooperate in different fields — all the more so since all of us are worried today by the escalation in the threat of nuclear conflict, by the arms race.

We have a need — a real necessity — for such exchanges and for discussing various questions. And I think that France is a very important partner for the Soviet Union in this sense. It is proceeding from these considerations and from this understanding that we are going to France.

Question: Mr. General Secretary, Soviet-French relations undoubtedly saw a period of cooling — I mean the years 1983 and 1984. Was this an interim thing, now a thing of the past, or will something of it survive?

Answer: Let us look ahead and fill our relations, our political dialogue, our economic and trade cooperation, and our cultural exchanges with new content, broaden our cooperation, find and identify common interests and possibilities for joint or parallel actions in the interests of France and the Soviet Union, in the interests of the other nations.

You know, way back in 1922, Vladimir I. Lenin said words that I have written down and decided to quote to you today. Perhaps I should have done so when I answered your first question, why we are going to France. Lenin said in 1922: "Any rapprochement with France is extremely desirable for us...." I think that the meaning of these words of Lenin and of the idea carried by them effectively holds just as true today.

Question: Regardless of what government France will have?

Answer: You know, every nation decides for itself what government to have, and, respecting the sovereignty — the sovereign right of every nation — we must reckon with it in our foreign policy. We have much trust and respect for the friendly people of France and will seek to maintain and develop relations with the incumbent government and with any government that may come into office tomorrow.

There are periods in relations between states when something darkens. In our case, when we discuss Soviet-French relations, I would concentrate more on what brings our peoples closer together. I think that this is the capital that enables us to build confidently on today's relations, to look ahead confidently and invigorate our relations. This, I think, will promote both the interests of our countries and the cause of peace. Let us look forward.

Question: You met with Mr. Marchais recently. Is it not paradoxical that at a time when the French Communists have withdrawn from the government and when they are criticizing the French government, you are paying your first visit to Mr. Mitterrand in France?

Answer: I do not think it is. What is taking place in France is the business of the French, their internal affairs. I know that those political forces that are governing the country today—I mean the Socialist Party and those who are allied with it—and also those who are in opposition, stand, to some extent or other, for the development of Soviet-French relations on the basis of traditions, on the basis of experience accumulated over the years. I think that it is a responsible position. Our approach is the same.

Question: It seems you have excellent relations with all the Social Democratic governments in Europe, don't you?

Answer: We have been cooperating energetically with Social Democratic parties during the past few years on matters that today are worrying the peoples of the world—I mean questions of war and peace. You must have noted that meetings with delegations of Socialist and Social Democratic parties have accounted for a sizable share of my meetings and talks during the past few months.

We think that our ideological differences are no obstacle to cooperation in tackling such urgent issues as those of war and peace, and we, for our part, say so openly. We have good relations and maintain useful contacts with the Social Democrats in West Germany, Sweden, and Finland, and with the Socialist parties of Japan and Austria. Generally speaking, we are open for cooperation with all the forces that have an interest in reversing the dangerous tendencies in the world situation and an interest in leading the world onto the road of cooperation, interaction, and mutual understanding.

Question: You seem to have been showing special interest in Europe lately. Is this a true impression?

Answer: The Soviet leadership has always kept sight of our relations with Western European countries in pursuing its foreign policy — I would even say, has kept them in the focus of attention.

This is understandable. You and we live in this Europe. I think that Western European countries have no less interest in developing relations with the Soviet Union and that the Soviet Union is no less prominent in their foreign policies than they are in Soviet foreign policy. We have some traditions. We have a history from which we draw some lessons, from which we are learning. Europeans will not be found wanting in wisdom. Whatever aspect of the development of human civilization we take, the contribution made by Europeans is immense. We live in the same house, though some use one entrance and others, another. We need to cooperate and develop communications within that house. I think it natural that the Soviet Union attaches much importance to this cooperation.

Question: A Gaullist approach?

Answer: I will not debate with you now over who should be credited with precedent. The question of interaction, cooperation, and establishment of relations with Western European countries has always played a substantial role in Soviet foreign policy. It was so long before Charles de Gaulle, that major political figure, emerged.

Question: Yet reaction to the actions of Western countries may vary. Indeed, when some officials of Soviet institutions were accused of spying and asked to leave France, no special reaction came from the Soviet Union, but when the British recently charged a group of Soviet officials with spying, the reaction of the Soviet side was strong and energetic. One has gotten the impression that the Soviet side acts according to the principle "an eye for an eye, a tooth for a tooth." Do you divide the Europeans into good and bad?

Answer: I think you will reserve for the Soviet Union the sovereign right to make decisions on each case as it sees fit. In so doing, we take into account both the interests of the Soviet Union and the over-all situation.

Question: What do you think of the European project known as "Eureka"?

Answer: I want to go to Paris and to learn in detail about "Eureka." Perhaps later we will continue an exchange of opinions on this question.

Question: Speaking a priori, do you prefer the "Eureka" project to the "Star Wars" plans of the Strategic Defense Initiative?

Answer: A priori, we prefer the nonmilitarization of space to its militarization. This is the main thing. If the "Eureka" project is pursuing peaceful goals — and this is just what we want to clarify in our conversations with the President and other French officials — we will think over our attitude to that project.

Question: You have written a letter to President Reagan. Have you put forward any new proposals?

Answer: Yes, we have.

Question: Could you tell us anything about these new proposals?

Answer: I think the Americans have already spoken about the main issues. They always call upon us to do everything in a confidential form, but their patience lasts only as long as a meeting lasts. As soon as contact is over, the world learns within ten minutes what has taken place at that "confidential meeting." At the least, the world gets the basics. That is why you must already have an idea on this matter. But I think that we will yet have discussions in France on this subject.

Question: What all this amounts to is a 40 percent reduction in nuclear arms arsenals, does it not?

Answer: I'd put off answering that question. These problems are now being presented in Geneva, and I would not like to answer your question before our delegation to the Geneva talks has presented our proposals in their entirety.

Question: Do you think that your forthcoming meeting with President Reagan in Geneva in a few weeks can become something more than just a getting-to-know-you?

Answer: It would be too great a luxury for the leaders of such countries as the Soviet Union and the United States of America, in today's tense situation, with the peoples of the world expecting definite, constructive steps primarily from the great powers, to go to Geneva just to exchange a handshake, to look at each other and to smile pleasantly in front of TV cameras. We invite our partners — I mean the President of the United States of America and his colleagues — to make thorough preparations for our meeting in Geneva — to lay, as soon as possible, during those preparations and at the meeting itself, solid bricks in the edifice of future peace. We must build peace — but a different peace and different relations — proceeding from realities. We have our interests, France has hers, and the United States of America has its interests. But who can say that the other nations of the world have no interests? And all those interests are coming across each other on the world scene. To think that only one country or group of countries can act on that scene means to have a wrong idea of today's world. I think that much is caused by this lack of comprehension. Realities must be reckoned with: They are a serious matter.

Question: Mr. General Secretary, lately you have been showing some signs of pessimism. You said in your address to the French people that the threat of nuclear catastrophe is not abating. You also said in one of your interviews earlier that perhaps it would be too late, and that the world situation was growing explosive. Talking in this way, you had in mind mostly the SDI. But the SDI as yet is a thing of the future. Why, then, do you think that the threat to peace now is graver than it was?

Answer: This is the most crucial question which must be answered precisely now.

When we say that we have reached a point beyond which events may get out of hand, it is not a sign of pessimism, it is a manifestation of the responsibility of the Soviet state and its leadership for the destiny of peace. There are those who stand to lose if the peoples grasp the situation as it is, but we have now reached a pont as a result of scientific and technological progress when the arms race can spill over into space. We have reached a point when weapons of new types — not even nuclear, but no less awesome and efficient, if we may talk about efficiency in such a case — can be developed.

Frankly, right now it is difficult enough to begin talks. You must have noticed that a sort of militarization of political consciousness is taking place. And what happens if the militarization of space begins tomorrow and if space-strike weapons are developed? What should the logical answer of the other side to such actions be? By no means a beginning to disarmament in strategic weapons and other nuclear systems. We should face realities squarely and see how the situation is shaping up. These are very serious matters, and they must not be camouflaged with demagoguery. If you'll excuse my saying so as a matter of fact, the destiny of the peoples – the destiny of peace – is at stake. There may emerge processes which will altogether block possibilities for seeking a peaceful settlement to problems. Ways must be looked for to counter that challenge.

If anyone introduces weapons into space, such constraints as the ABM Treaty, the accord on the limitation of strategic weapons, and others will go overboard. That is why we have really approached a very critical point in the development of the international situation. It is not a pessimistic position, but a realistic appraisal of a real situation. And it prompts a need to look for solutions to lead the development of international relations onto a different road, onto the path of peaceful cooperation; to stop the arms race; to begin reductions in nuclear armaments; and eventually to eliminate them. And I must say that the matter hinges not only on the position of the Soviet Union and the United States of America – other countries also bear responsibility. Today one cannot sit it out on the sidelines: One must take a stand. The times demand that every responsible government or politician destined, so to speak, to lead one state or another should today take a clear stand on these issues.

Question: You have been General Secretary of the CPSU Central Committee for several months now. Some people view you as a leader for the next quarter of a century. What would you like to change in the Soviet Union right now?

Answer: I can hardly add anything to what I have already said and what is known in France. We view the situation in the country as follows. On the one hand, we have traveled a great road and made immense economic, social, and political progress. In a historically short period, we have managed to carry out major plans and introduce radical changes in a vast country, once backward in terms of economy and education, and populated by many peoples. But we can no longer be satisfied with this progress. Perhaps this attitude is logical if we bear in mind that as man develops, his needs—material, cultural, and intellectual—keep growing. Our society must change to meet these needs to an ever-growing dynamism in the economy, in the social and the cultural and intellectual spheres. This is the main goal toward which we are working now.

Question: You are seen by many as a man of change. Why, then, are there no changes in the Soviet Union on a matter that, we believe, is damaging the reputation of the Soviet Union abroad, namely, human rights.

The names of Sakharov and Scharansky are mentioned in France, and a campaign is being conducted so that Soviet Jews could leave the country if they wish. Why not take all this into account?

Answer: I could put it as follows: Let us in the Soviet Union manage our affairs ourselves, and you in France manage yours. But I will nevertheless answer your question. The issue of human rights is no problem for us, and we are ready to debate it anywhere, in front of any audience, and with any representatives. We have plenty to say on this issue that is now being played up artificially by Western propaganda and exploited to poison relations between nations and states.

As regards economic and social rights, we could demonstrate the state in which they are in the most developed Western countries, including France, and the situation in our country. Relevant facts are common knowledge. As for political rights, I could say that our Supreme Soviet has more worker and peasant deputies than all the parliaments of the developed capitalist countries put together. It would be interesting to stage an experiment, at least for half a year or for a year, and send workers to the parliaments of your countries. We would then see what happens. But workers, as a rule, are kept away—yet, in our country, they are in key positions everywhere, from rural Soviets to the Supreme Soviet.

Of course, we have people that by some logic or another have fallen out with the Soviet form of government, with socialism, and profess some different ideology. Problems in such cases arise when one individual or another comes into conflict with the law. That was what happened to the Scharansky mentioned by you. He breached our laws and was sentenced by a court for that.

You mentioned the "Jewish question." I would be glad to hear of Jews enjoying anywhere such political and other rights as they have in our country. The Jewish population, which accounts for 0.69 percent of the entire population of the country, are represented in its political and cultural life on a scale of at least 10 to 20 percent. Many of them are people well known countrywide.

When it is a question of reunification of families, we agree to this and settle such questions. There are exceptions when individuals in question know state secrets. But does not France have legislation protecting the interests of the state? It does. I know so. We will continue to resolve these questions without fuss, through a humanitarian approach.

Question: And a last question, just in passing: Is it true that there are four million political prisoners in the Soviet Union?

Answer: Absurd! It calls to mind, you know, Goebbels's propaganda. I am amazed that you, Mr. Mourousi, an educated and up-to-date man, could ask such a question. I repeat: It is absurd.

Question: Mr. Gorvachev, you seem to be practicing a new method of communication, a new method of leadership. Is there a "Gorbachev style"? If so, how would you define that style?

Answer: I think there is no "Gerbachev style." I have already said so. As to our methods of work—particularly the style of my work—it is not something that appeared yesterday or a month, two, or three ago. I have been working like this all my life. And many of my comrades have been working precisely the same way.

The style we are cultivating in our party we define as a Leninist style of work. It is characterized by such things as extensive communication with the working people, publicizing our work, and analysis of the real processes that underlie policy-making. It is everything that Lenin taught our party. I am an enthusiastic champion of precisely such an approach. The example set by Lenin is the best possible example. We are following the road of Lenin and using his style.

Question: A new generation of Soviet leaders has risen to power with you, Mr. Gorbachev. For instance, at the end of last week, we heard that the Soviet Head of Government had been replaced. What can this new generation of Soviet leaders give your country in addition to style?

Answer: I think what is taking place is a normal process. There is nothing out-of-the-ordinary in it. Every generation makes its contribution to progress, to molding political, cultural, and intellectual values. I think that the present generation of leaders in the Soviet Union will make their contribution. This will concern primarily large-scale work to upgrade socialism. We know what is to be done to bring out to a fuller extent the best aspects inherent in that social system. And it is man with his needs who is the centerpiece of all our aspirations.

Every effort will be taken to make our economic system, our political system, the system of socialist democracy more dynamic. Our attention—the most rapt attention possible—will be devoted particularly to bringing out the importance of the human factor in full measure.

Question: You come to Paris the day after tomorrow. If you have an evening off, what would you prefer? Going to the Picasso Museum, seeing Shakespeare's *Julius Caesar,* a concert, an opera? In short, what is your preference?

Answer: Since I know the program and since it does not give me an evening off—let alone a day off—I have no such problem.

But generally speaking, when you visit another country, it is always interesting to learn about its past, too. But I must say that I have no less interest—or even more interest—in the present-day life of every society, every country, every people, their problems, traditions and interests. Perhaps this is natural for a politician.

Question: Mr. General Secretary, probably we would have a thousand other questions, but we must conclude our interview. We want to thank you again for granting this exclusive interview to French television.

Answer: I was happy to meet with representatives of French television. I think our conversation with you makes it possible to say that we can meet, that we can discuss all matters calmly.

We are interested in further development of relations with the friendly people of France. This is a matter that requires reciprocity.

We must move toward each other. It is from such a viewpoint that we regard our forthcoming visit, too. This is a good opportunity for upgrading our relations and showing the prospects for them for the future.

September 30, 1985

37

MESSAGE OF GREETINGS TO THE FIRST INTERNATIONAL CONGRESS OF THE ASSOCIATION OF THE PARTICIPANTS IN SPACE FLIGHTS

I WANT to convey my friendly greetings to the First International Congress of an Association of the Participants in Space Flights. The very fact of the convocation of your congress is symbolic. It indicates that mankind enters the space era vigorously. The number of people who know what space is not by hearsay but from their own experience, and who have cast a glance around our entire beautiful planet, is growing. It is natural that when matters concern space affairs, your voice is heeded. It is important, of course, that this voice sound in favor of peace both on earth and in space.

It is no secret to anyone that man's going out into space, which has been the realization of his cherished dream, may turn out to be, paradoxically it may seem, a mortal threat. The Soviet Union firmly comes out in favor of preventing a tragic course of events. Our alternative is close international cooperation in the peaceful exploration and use of outer space for the benefit of the whole of mankind.

You are already part of twentieth-century history. The more tangible your contribution to serving the cause of peace, the greater the cooperation and mutual understanding among peoples can be.

I wholeheartedly wish success and well-being to the participants in the congress.

Mikhail Gorbachev
October 3, 1985

38

ADDRESS
TO
FRENCH
PARLIAMENTARIANS

PARIS. Mikhail Gorbachev, General Secretary of the CPSU Central Committee and member of the Presidium of the Supreme Soviet of the USSR, met today with French Members of Parliament, members of the Foreign Affairs Committees, and Franco-Soviet Friendship Groups of the National Assembly and the Senate at Lassay Palace.

E. A. Shevardnadze, Member of the Politburo of the CPSU Central Committee and Minister of Foreign Affairs of the USSR; I. V. Arkhipov, First Vice Chairman of the USSR Council of Ministers; N. D. Komarov, First Deputy Minister of Foreign Trade of the USSR, Y. P. Velikhov, Vice President of the USSR Academy of Sciences; members of the Foreign Affairs Commissions of the Chambers of the USSR Supreme Soviet A. M. Alexandrov, V. V. Zagladin and L. M. Zamyatin; Deputy Minister of Foreign Affairs of the USSR A. G. Kovalev; and USSR Ambassador to France Y. M. Vorontsov were present at the meeting on the Soviet side.

Mikhail Gorbachev was greeted warmly by Louis Mermaz, President of the National Assembly of France, and Alain Poher, President of the French Senate.

In his speech, Louis Mermaz pointed out the long-standing traditions of friendship and cooperation between the two countries. Cooperation between France and the Soviet Union has been and remains an example that must inspire countries with different socio-economic systems, he said. Our people fought side-by-side during the years of World War II. This strengthened our friendship. In the 1960s Franco-Soviet relations to a great extent promoted the commencement of the spirit of Helsinki. Our cooperation has been and can be of great mutual benefit in the future and contribute to the progress of the peoples of France and the Soviet Union, and of the whole of mankind.

We sincerely believe in the Soviet Union's striving for peace. It is with great interest that we are studying your proposals on a moratorium on nuclear tests and on the United States and the Soviet Union reducing by 50 percent their nuclear arms capable of reaching each other's territory, because we have always held that the two great nuclear powers should set the example in this field.

The contacts maintained by members of the parliaments of the two countries over many years have facilitated the strengthening of Franco-Soviet relations, Louis Marmaz pointed out. Good relations between France and the Soviet Union will facilitate, to a certain extent, the favorable development of events in Europe and beyond. The French Members of Parliament are prepared to continue direct and constructive dialogue.

Then the Members of Parliament were addressed by Mikhail Gorbachev.

Esteemed Presidents,
Esteemed Deputies and Senators,
Ladies and Gentlemen,
I am gratified by the opportunity to address the French Parliament, to meet with you—the elected representatives of the French people. I would like to avail myself of this opportunity to thank the President of the Republic for his kind invitation to visit your country.

Today is the second day of our delegation's visit. Important meetings have been held and an exchange of views has been started on topical questions of bilateral relations and international affairs. Of course, as yet it is too early to sum up the results of the talks with President Mitterrand and other French statesmen. But it is already obvious that both sides are showing a desire to impart a new impulse to the development of relations between our countries and, considering the existing realities, to bring closer our positions on international problems.

In talking with the President of the Republic and addressing you today, I strive naturally for the essence, the main direction of the Soviet state's foreign policy to be understood better and more fully in France. Like the foreign policy of any state, it is determined first of all by internal requirements.

Permit me to dwell briefly on this question. I believe you know what a long and, in many respects, difficult road has been traversed by my country in the years of Soviet government. From Czarist Russia we inherited extreme economic backwardness. Within a very short period of time, if the yardstick of history is applied, the Soviet Union has turned into a mighty — in all respects, modern — power with a high level of popular culture. We put an end to unemployment and ensured for the population such social boons as free provision of housing, medical services, and education. I will cite a few figures illustrating our country's economic development. In the years since the war alone, our national income has grown more than 16 times and industrial output, 24 times. In the same period, the real income of Soviet people has sextupled.

Pride in our success does not make us complacent. We see that at the present stage society's increased maturity sets before us much more far-ranging tasks, which, in many ways, are new ones by their content. We are fully aware also of the shortcomings that exist in our work, of the existing difficulties and problems, quite often sufficiently serious ones. The main task that we set ourselves today can be expressed in a brief formula: to accelerate society's social and economic development.

This goal requires that many things be raised to a higher level — the scientific and technical base of the national economy, the methods of management and people themselves, their awareness, skills, and qualifications. In short, we have set off on a road to achieving a new qualitative state in society.

Our main task is to make the economy more efficient and dynamic, to make the lives of people spiritually richer, more complete and meaningful, to develop the system of socialist self-government by the people.

It is not difficult to understand that not only reliable peace, but a calm, normal international situation are paramount conditions for attaining these ends. And it is these priorities that determine our foreign policy; a policy in which, naturally, we strive to take account in full measure of the interests and requirements of other peoples, all the realities of the present epoch.

Our world, a multifaceted and contradictory world, is rapidly approaching the end of the century and the millennium. It has more than its fair share of complex problems of political, economic and social nature. The coexistence on our planet of two social systems, each of which is living and developing according to its own laws, has long become a reality.

But we must see the other reality as well. And that reality is that the interconnection and interdependence of countries and continents is becoming increasingly closer. This is an inevitable condition of the development of the world economy, of scientific and technological progress, the acceleration of the exchange of information and the movement of people and things — on the earth and even in space. In short, the entire development of human civilization is becoming more interconnected.

Alas, it is not always that the gains of civilization are a boon for people. All too often and too vigorously, the achievements of science and technology are also being used for the creation of means of annihilating human beings, for the development and stockpiling of ever more terrible types of weapons.

In these conditions, Hamlet's famous question — "To be or not to be" — is already being set not before a single individual, but before mankind. It develops into a global problem. There can be only one answer: Mankind, civilization must survive at all costs. But our survival can be ensured only if we learn to live together, to get along on this small planet by mastering the difficult art of showing consideration for each other's interests. This we call the policy of peaceful coexistence.

We are strong enough to give crushing rebuff to any attempts to encroach on our people's security and peaceful work. Yet we hold that it is not by force of arms, but only and exclusively by force of example that one must prove the correctness of one's ideology, the advantages of the system that each people has chosen of its own free will. Such is our firm conviction.

I spoke yesterday to the President about our perception of the main axis of contradictions, the struggle of the two tendencies in world politics. We regard as extremely dangerous the view, no matter how it is being justified, that the tasks facing the international community can be solved by the creation and stockpiling of ever-new and more destructive types of arms: on earth and in space. We also regard as dangerous actions that preserve and aggravate international tension. The latter is incandescent as it is — so incandescent that it has now become extremely difficult to reach agreement not only on complex, urgent matters but even on relatively simple problems. If we do not stop the present tendencies, tomorrow we will not be able to overcome their monstrous inertia. It will become even more difficult to talk.

That is why we consider it so important right now, immediately, before it is too late, to stop the "infernal train" of the arms race, to start reduction of arms, improve the international situation, and develop peaceful cooperation among peoples. This is a mutual interest: This is everybody's task. Nobody can permit himself to sit it out on the sidelines.

The Soviet Union, as you probably know, has not only been issuing calls, but has also been acting along these lines.

We have suspended further deployment of medium-range missiles in Europe unilaterally and have called on the United States to respond in kind. We have stopped all nuclear explosions and called on the United States to respond in kind. Quite naturally, we address this call to the other nuclear powers as well.

The Soviet Union proposes a start in the reduction of armed forces and armaments of both sides in Central Europe, and to begin with a reduction in Soviet and American troops. Moreover, we are prepared to reduce more troops than the Americans.

As for space, we are for its use exclusively for peaceful purposes and call persistently for the reaching of agreement on this issue because a transfer of the arms race into space will make reduction of nuclear arsenals objectively impossible. As you know, we have submitted to the United Nations a proposal on international cooperation in the peaceful exploration of outer space.

And now I would like to inform you of the new steps taken by the Soviet Union. They pursue the same aim: to stop the baleful process of the arms race and ward off the war danger hanging over mankind.

First: A few days ago, we proposed to the Government of the United States of America to come to terms on total prohibition of space-strike arms for both sides and to reduce really radically — by 50 percent — the nuclear arms capable of reaching each other's territory.

In other words, we propose a practical solution to the very same tasks that were agreed upon by both sides early this year as being the aims of the Geneva talks: not only to stop the arms race, but to lower the level of armaments drastically and at the same time avert an arms race in space.

There is hardly any need to say how all this would strengthen strategic stability and mutual trust.

I can inform you that our delegation in Geneva has been instructed to present concrete proposals on this question and has been authorized to give the participants exhaustive explanations.

I am saying all this because a multitude of versions and false rumors are already circulating in the West concerning our proposal, and it is time for some clarification.

Second. Concerning medium-range nuclear weapons in Europe. With the aim of making easier agreement on their speediest mutual reduction (as we are often told, in Western Europe, too, there is great interest in this), we consider it possible to conclude a corresponding agreement separately, outside of direct connection with the problem of space and strategic arms. This road, as it appears to us, may turn out to be practical.

In this context, I consider it important to explain our position on such an issue as the role of the nuclear potential of France and Britain in the European balance of forces. This potential is growing rapidly, and we can no longer ignore it. It was said from the French side that the nuclear forces of France are not subject to discussion without her participation. This stands to reason. It follows from this that it is time to start direct dialogue between us on this theme and try to find an acceptable way out through joint effort. Of course, the Soviet Union is prepared for such a direct dialogue with France, just as with Britain.

I want to stress at this point that we will consider the security interests of France in the most attentive manner. And today, as it appears to us, the question of a reduction in her armaments is not on the agenda.

Third. You know that we have announced a moratorium on deployment of medium-range missiles in Europe. The number of SS-20 missiles that the Soviet Union has standing ready in the

European Zone is now 243. This means that it accords precisely with the level of June 1984, when the additional deployment of our missiles was started in response to the deployment of American medium-range missiles in Europe. The SS-20 missiles that were deployed additionally in the process have been withdrawn from stand-ready, and the stationary installations that housed these missiles will be dismantled within the next two months. This is verifiable. As to our reply measures in respect to the territory of the United States itself, they continue to remain in force.

I would also like to explain the meaning that we give to the term "European Zone." This is the zone in which medium-range missiles capable of striking targets on the territory of Western Europe are deployed.

It should be noted that we have already totally phased out the old and very powerful SS-5 missiles and are continuing to phase out the SS-4 missiles. This means that, on the whole, the number of medium-range carrier missiles in the European Zone of the Soviet Union is now much smaller than ten or even fifteen years ago. In accepting this self-limitation, we proceed from the broad interests of European security. I think that Europe is now entitled to expect a move in response by the United States—the termination by it of further deployment of its medium-range missiles on the continent of Europe.

You see what serious steps the Soviet Union is taking. In combination with our previous actions, our latest proposals, as it seems to us, are a package of constructive and realistic measures that would bring about a genuine breakthrough in the development of international relations. A breakthrough in favor of peace, security, and cooperation among nations.

This, if you please, is our program for improving the explosive international situation that threatens peace. We expect that in response to our proposals, the West, too, will traverse its part of the road.

I should like to stress that the realization of the program proposed by us would also signify substantial advance toward an aim that is so desired by all nations and is so important to them: prohibition and total liquidation of nuclear arms and total delivery of mankind from the threat of nuclear war.

There can be no victors in a nuclear war. It seems that all responsible politicians are in agreement on this point. It is high time to draw a practical conclusion from this: to stop the nuclear arms race. And we believe that this demand will be supported by all honest, realistically thinking political forces, public figures, all people who cherish their homeland, their lives, the lives of their children and grandchildren.

The task of totally prohibiting chemical weapons and liquidating their stockpiles is becoming ever more urgent. At the Conference on Disarmament in Geneva, the Soviet Union is participating actively in the drafting of a relevant convention. We are meeting our partners in the talks halfway on a number of substantial aspects, including verification. I am sure that it is quite possible to reach agreement on reliable verification.

Incidentally, the following thought also prompts itself. If we reached agreement on the nonproliferation of nuclear arms, why not apply the same method to chemical weapons? This task would be in the general channel of efforts to achieve a total ban on them. The Soviet Union would be prepared to take part in the drafting of an international accord on the nonproliferation of chemical weapons. We are also prepared to do everything in our power for the creation of a zone free from chemical weapons in the center of Europe.

As I speak here in Paris, in the heart, it can be said, of Western Europe, I cannot but speak about some substantial problems of European security, about how we in the Soviet Union view them.

I will start with the most general question. What, after all, is security in Europe? It is the absence of war and the threat of war. The interdependence, the intertwining of the destinies of peoples despite the difference of the social roads chosen by them, is felt in Europe with special force. Because of geographical density and oversaturation with armaments, Europe, like no other continent, is vulnerable to armed conflict — the more so, nuclear weapons.

This means that Europe's security cannot be ensured by military means, by military force. This is an absolutely new situation and means a departure from traditions, from a mentality and manner of action that took centuries—even milleniums to form. Human thought does not adjust to something new right away. This applies to all of us. We feel this. We have started a rethinking and an adjusting in full conformity with the new realities on many customary problems, including the military and political spheres. We would also want such a rethinking to take place in Western Europe and beyond.

So far, fear of unacceptable retribution is one of the obstacles to war, to the use of military force. Everybody understands, though, that lasting peace cannot be built on fear alone. But the entire question is: Where should one search for the alternative to fear, or, to use military language, deterrence?

We see what attempts are now being made to find a way out— by using new arms in the so-called "Star Wars." This is an illusion, and an extremely dangerous one at that. It is naïve, in general, to search for a solution to the problem of security in the perfection of shield and sword. Security in Europe, just as international security as a whole, can be achieved only on the road of peaceful coexistence, relaxation of tension, disarmament, strengthening of trust, and development of international cooperation.

This is a long and difficult road, the more so that it requires the overcoming of mutual suspicions, mistrust, and prejudices accumulated over decades. But there is no other road if we want to live. And, like any long road, it begins with the first steps, which often are the most difficult to make. We understand this and want to help ensure solution of the task—for ourselves and for you. It is this desire that motivates the proposals that I have already mentioned.

This desire for peace applies also to the conference in Stockholm, which is discussing the important problem of mutual trust in military matters. As it appears to us, the contours of future accords are gradually beginning to take shape there. They include making more definite and imparting maximum effectiveness to the principle of not using force. They comprise a definite set of confidence-building measures in the military field—what we might call safety fuses to prevent an erroneous interpretation of the actions of the other side under conditions of aggravating military confrontation. A number of states—first of all, neutral ones—propose agreement on mutual exchanges of annual plans for military activity, subject to notification. We are prepared for such an accord in the hopes that it will help overcome suspicion and impede covert preparations for war.

The ideas of setting up nuclear-free zones in various parts of the world, including our continent—in the north of Europe and in the Balkans—are spreading ever wider. We support these ideas and are ready to take part in the appropriate guarantees where they are required. We view as useful the idea of creating a corridor free of nuclear arms along both sides of the line dividing the two military-political groupings. We also hold that nations that do not possess nuclear arms and do not have them on their territory have full right to reliable guarantees of security based on international law, guarantees that nuclear arms will not be used against them.

Many aspects of European cooperation are recorded in the Helsinki Final Act. We hold that it is a serious achievement and retains its importance fully. When the tenth anniversary of the Helsinki Accords was marked, all the participants in the All-European process came out for its continuation. The Soviet Union is prepared to take the most vigorous part in this continuation.

Every European country has contributed a share of its national experience to the Helsinki process. This is a common asset of the peoples of Europe, and it should be protected and multiplied by joint effort.

The political climate in Europe depends in no small measure on the development of economic ties between West and East. Here, too, an innovative approach is needed. The reaching of the targets for industrial, technical, and scientific progress that face each country today could be made much easier by effective international division of labor. We in the Soviet Union are ready for this cooperation, and for a search for new forms of coproduction and cooperation. It goes without saying that this implies principles of mutual advantage, equality, and a serious approach.

The establishment of more businesslike relations between the CMEA and the EEC also appears to us useful. The countries of the Council for Mutual Economic Assistance have displayed in this respect a constructive initiative, which appears to have been met favorably. It is important for it to produce concrete results. Here, as has already been stated, in the measure in which the EEC countries act as a "political unit," we are prepared to find a common tongue with them on definite international problems as well. This arrangement could be made in various forms, including parliamentary ties, among them with those who represent the European Parliament.

Without all European countries uniting efforts, it will not be possible really to solve either such an acute problem as preserving and improving the environment on our continent. In many of its areas, figuratively speaking, the land is beginning to burn under our feet, the rain falling from the sky is acidic, if not fiery, while the sky itself cannot be seen because of smoke. European rivers and seas are becoming pitifully polluted. At one time, it seems, we all did not act with sufficient farsightedness and generated such problems that now simply defy solution within national frameworks. Here truly there is an area in which we all must become aware of our continent's common destiny.

Much can be done in the broad sphere that is called "humanitarian." The preservation by common effort of the cultural values of the past, cultural exchanges that mutually enrich one of the cradles of mankind's spiritual values — Europe — does this not deserve the closest attention? It is with interest that we are preparing for such an extraordinary event as the "cultural forum" opening in a few days in Budapest. In this sphere, too, lies expansion of information about each other's lifestyle, and cultivation of feelings of mutual sympathy and respect. The mutual study of each other's languages is of such importance from this point of view. Extensive exchanges of school pupils, students, and teachers is a promising area. It is very important for the young generations to have correct perceptions of each other because it is they who will build a peaceful Europe. The pooling of efforts in the struggle against disease — old and new — is a task of immense importance.

The Soviet Union attaches the most serious importance to human rights guarantees. All that is needed is to free this issue from hyprocrisy and speculation, from attempts at interference in the internal affairs of other countries. Such problems as the position of migrant workers, mixed marriages, and reunification of families stand rather acute in Europe today. We are for approaching such problems in a positive and humane spirit with full respect for the sovereign rights of all nations.

Ladies and Gentlemen,

I believe that in the present situation it is especially important not to emulate medieval fanatics and not to spread ideological differences to international relations. Stability in these relations, less susceptibility of them to political situations, will likewise consolidate stability in Europe as a whole.

We do not think, for instance, that there is an eternal taboo on contacts in some form between the Warsaw Treaty and the North Atlantic alliance as organizations, not to speak of overcoming Europe's division into opposing groupings in the more or less foreseeable future. As is known, this is exactly what we and our allies are proposing. But, as we see it, even in conditions of the existence of two blocs, it is possible to create such a *modus vivendi* as would blunt the acuteness of the present confrontation.

And, of course, it is important today—as never before—to develop more intensive political dialogue between East and West, to use all the already-established forms of such dialogue—regular meetings at various levels, including, of course, the highest, political consultations, broad contacts between the scientific and cultural communities.

We regard the development of parliamentary ties as a very important matter as well. I would like to emphasize this point especially as I am speaking within these walls. This includes, naturally, the development of parliamentary ties with France. The Deputies of the National Assembly and Senate of France can be assured that they are welcome guests in Moscow. I state this on behalf of the Supreme Soviet of the Soviet Union.

Such, in the most general outline, are our views on how really it is possible to achieve—and within a comparatively short period of time, at that—an improvement in the situation on our continent and to increase Europe's role in overcoming the present stretch of confrontation.

I will add yet another moment. The need for more active interaction to eliminate the seats of conflict and tension existing in various areas has never been greater than now. The fact that the

Soviet Union and France, despite their belonging to opposing
military-political groupings, have much in common in the approach
to a number of presently existing regional problems and situations is
one of the examples of opportunities for such interaction. For
instance, the situation in the Middle East, Central America, South
Africa, and so on. Our contacts with the French leaders confirm
this.

In proposing an expansion of good-neighborliness and cooperation with Western Europe, we have no intention at all of belittling
the importance of a possible contribution to this goal by Canada,
which belongs to NATO, and at the same time has signed the
Helsinki Final Act. Neither does our European policy have an anti-
American bias.

Since one hears much speculation on this theme, permit me to
look at it in greater detail. The very way the question is posed—that
by improving relations with Western Europe, we want to drive a
wedge, to set it at loggerheads with the United States—is absurd.
First, we want to have good relations not only with Western Europe,
but with the United States, just as, for that matter, also, with China,
Japan and other countries. We are not pursuing a Metternich-like
policy of "balance of power," of setting one state against another,
knocking together blocs and counterblocs, creating "axes" and
"triangles," but a policy of global détente, of strengthening world
security and developing universal international cooperation. Second, we are realists, and we understand how strong are the ties—
historical, political, and economic—linking Western Europe and
the United States.

Esteemed Deputies,

The best minds of mankind have warned about the danger of
our consciousness lagging behind rapid change in social being. This
is especially topical today. Man is beginning to explore the galaxy.
But how much remains undone on earth?

Not a single nation, not a single state is capable of solving the
existing problems alone. And the old baggage of disunity, confrontation, and mistrust impedes unification.

I know that far from everyone in this hall accepts our world
outlook, our ideology. As a realist, I am not trying to convert

anyone to our creed. Any philosophy is approached by individuals and peoples themselves, achieving it only through much suffering, only by accepting it with their minds and hearts. But despite all differences in political and philosophical views, in ideals and values, we must remember one thing: We all are keepers of the fire of life handed down to us by earlier generations.

Each had its own mission, and each, in its own way, enriched world civilization. The giants of the Renaissance and the great French Revolution, the heroes of the October Revolution in Russia, of victory and the Résistance — they all have fulfilled their duty to history.

And what about our generation? It has made great discoveries, but it has also found recipes for self-destruction of the human race. On the threshold of the third millennium, we must burn the black book of nuclear alchemy. May the twenty-first century become the first century of life without fear of universal death.

We will fulfill this mission if we unite our efforts. The Soviet Union is prepared to make its contribution to ensuring a peaceful, free and flourishing future for Europe and all the other continents. We will not stop our efforts for this.

October 3, 1985

JOINT PRESS CONFERENCE
WITH
FRANÇOIS MITTERRAND
IN PARIS

ON OCTOBER 4, 1985, a joint press conference of President François Mitterrand of France and Mikhail Gorbachev, General Secretary of the CPSU Central Committee, was opened by Francois Mitterrand in the Élysée Palace in Paris upon the completion of their talks. Mitterrand pointed out that it was with much interest that he had taken note of the whole package of issues set forth by Mikhail Gorbachev, and that he had carried away from the talks with the Soviet leader "the feeling that both sides have made progress in familiarizing themselves with their respective views and thus got the opportunity to contribute to progress in the resolution of the complex problems confronting the present-day world." François Mitterrand declared that states should orient themselves in their policy to détente in international relations, which have recently sharpened too often.

Having noted that the point at issue in the course of the French-Soviet talks was primarily that of disarmament, of an equilibrium of forces, and, consequently, of peace and conditions of preserving peace and of how to avert the risk of war, the French head of state made special mention of the new Soviet proposal for a 50 percent cut in all strategic weapons.

"The countries directly concerned—the United States and the Soviet Union—should discuss that proposal in more specific terms," the President said. "To this end they have all possibilities: experts and the necessary data. They can compare what is comparable; dispute what is disputable. In other words, the Soviet Union and the United States have everything necessary to ensure progress at the talks. I hope that this aim will be served by the meeting between the General Secretary of the CPSU Central Committee and the U.S. President next month.

"All, including those who do not take part in the Geneva talks, have a stake in their success, as peace is our common cause."

François Mitterrand pointed out that a considerable cut in arms could be achieved only if linked with the impermissibility of spreading the arms race to outer space. "France has always wished not to create differences with its allies, among whom are its American friends," the President said. "Quite recently France was forced to declare under well-known circumstances that it would not participate in any form in the development of space weapons. These weapons differ from the existing ones. The spread of nuclear weapons into outer space will signal not only an end to the treaty of 1972 on antiballistic missile systems, but also a new spiral of the arms race, and the advancement toward other forms of armament, which I cannot even specify at this moment.

"I certainly remember the statement that was made to me to this effect by the American leaders: They think of it as a defensive weapon, but I do not wish to discuss that. France has already said that she would not participate in the SDI program, that outer space is also of interest to her, but she believes that there are other methods of exploration of space and its use by mankind at the present stage."

President Mitterrand recalled that France had invariably declined that her nuclear weapons be taken into account and emphasized that France's nuclear forces are not to be discussed without her participation.

Mitterrand stated that the disarmament problem should be examined in all of its aspects simultaneously: not only in terms of medium-range nuclear weapons, but also in terms of strategy and in terms of the conventional weapons, and, what really matters, in terms of chemical weapons and antimissiles. "France is not against an exchange of views, in particular, with the Soviet Union, and the established or renewed dialogue is a good method for that." But he did not find it sensible to think that talks could be held.

"The position of our countries is not the same. We belong to two different types of society. We belong to different alliances. To overcome this distance, it is necessary to display mutual understanding and contribute toward all opportunities for broadening cooperation. This is precisely what we have done and will continue doing since the General Secretary has kindly invited us to visit Moscow next year, and I have accepted this invitation.

"Other problems have certainly been dealt with," the President continued, "in particular, our wish that the Stockholm conference should end before the middle of next year with an accord between its

35 participating countries and the wish that the Helsinki Final Act should be implemented in its various aspects to a larger degree than has been the case until now.

"We have touched upon some most important aspects of what could be called regional conflicts," François Mitterrand pointed out.

"In terms of bilateral relations, our conversations covered trade, equilibrium of the trade balance, a number of projects in the field that could be described as peaceful exploration of outer space, and exceptional successes in the field of technology.

"We have spoken, in particular, about what is called nuclear fusion—a field in which our two countries have advanced technology—in short, touched upon all fields where one or the other side has to its credit some accomplishments, wealth and successes from which mutual benefit could be derived."

In conclusion, François Mitterrand said, "I would like all my pronouncements to be received as gratitude of sorts for our discussing seriously the world's most important problems, and also for the General Secretary conducting these discussions in such a way that makes it possible to envision even more cordial cooperation. This would well accord with the historical traditions of our two countries throughout all times and especially after the Second World War, in which the Soviet Union, and we, too, suffered such heavy loses. Once again, we thank the peoples of the Soviet Union for their sacrifices, one of the heroic results of which was the liberation of France."

Then Mikhail Gorbachev made a statement:

"Mr. President, I think at this point I can take over from you. I would like to say again why and for what we have come to France. We in the Soviet Union proceed from the premise that the present situation in the world is at such a stage of development when responsible decisions and responsible actions are needed, first of all by countries with considerable international weight. I have in mind the Soviet Union, the United States, France, and Britain, and other countries. The realities of the world today are such that we can build a better, safer world, ensure progress, and achieve an improvement in the international situation if all this becomes our common endeavor.

For all the differences in our political systems, ideologies, and world outlooks we all face the need to find a road to such a world characterized by trust, actual understanding and cooperation. We are for dialogue. In any case, the Soviet leadership is of the opinion that all this is simply common sense.

For the Soviet Union, France is an important partner for discussing such questions. And these traditions nourish our present relations. I think they will nourish our relations in the future as well. When I speak of traditions, I mean not only contacts of a political nature, on the level of state leadership. I mean, first of all, what for decades and centuries has already united our peoples.

This is the solid foundation that has always enabled Russia and France, and the Soviet Union and France to meet at the most difficult periods in human history and discuss the most acute, vitally important problems, to engage in a search for solutions to such problems. It is exactly proceeding from this that we accepted President François Mitterrand's invitation to visit France. I want to express to you once again heartfelt gratitude for your hospitality.

To what you have said, I would add that our countries, both before and during the visit—and it is already nearing its end—were and remain true to their sociopolitical systems, each professing their own ideology and belonging today to the same military-political alliances to which they belonged yesterday and to which they will belong tomorrow. Neither I nor the President ever set the task of converting each other to the other creed in the course of the talks.

But does the fact that we belong to different systems and military-political organizations diminish the importance of the dialogue in which the Soviet Union and France, the General Secretary and the President, are engaged?

I think, perhaps, in a certain sense this even has its advantages. And this conclusion is confirmed by what the President has said in the talks and meetings held during these days—and we had three meetings with the President face-to-face, not to speak of the conversations with other French politicians. It is very important that this echoes the President's thought. Each in his real situation, the leaders of the Soviet Union and France, have managed to rise above the existing differences and analyze the processes taking place in the world, compare their evaluations, exchange views on what the contribution of the Soviet Union and France could be to making the events in the world and the international situation change for the better. I think this is evidence of the existence of an immense sense of responsibility both on the part of the Soviet leaders and the leaders of France for the destiny of the world. And this, I think, is quite important for conducting the dialogue and outlining ways of joint or parallel actions to improve the situation in the world.

We generally have a high opinion of the talks of the past few days with President Mitterrand and other French statesmen and politicians. These were substantive conversations, noted by a constructive character. They actually took place in an open form and in a spirit of mutual respect and goodwill.

The President has already touched upon the problems covered in those conversations. They were centered on the more urgent problems of the present dangerous international situation. We have quite understandable differences on a number of definite issues, but there also emerged a common understanding of the need to do everything possible to improve the situation, to remove the threat looming over the peoples, and to contribute to a turn from confrontation to détente. I am convinced that the President shares this point of view.

The President has said that the word "détente" featured in our talks not because we indulged in reminiscences of the past. This is a certain lesson in the process of détente. We will not now go into reasons why that process has been weakened and subverted to some extent. All of us have realized the urgent need to return to détente if we want to think big and approach matters of safeguarding peace with great responsibility. In this context, the realistic possibility to return to détente has been mentioned here and also in the course of our talks on détente.

Questions of how to put an end to the unprecedented arms race were the most important in our conversations. In Paris we informed the President, the Parliament, the public, and the people of France of the proposals that we made to the leadership of the United States

of America and that have already become a subject of study at the
Geneva talks. These questions are of concern not only to the leaders
of France and the Soviet Union; they are of concern to all nations,
all sober-minded political leaders, all those who have not become
insanely obsessed with the arms race, confrontation, and hostility.

I am not going to repeat our new proposals. You are familiar
with them. I would merely like to say that after our exchange of
views — and it was a very substantial one — the leaders of France and
their President expressed understanding of the importance of our
proposals, their constructive potential. When we made these proposals, we realized what the Soviet leadership has been stating over
the past several months. The Soviet Union is prepared for radical
reductions in nuclear arms if space-strike arms are kept out of
space. This is the crux of the problem. The way the question is
posed is in line with the January accords between the Minister of
Foreign Affairs of the Soviet Union and the Secretary of State of the
United States.

Several weeks and months ago, our partners in the Geneva
talks were saying, "Where are your radical proposals?" Information
on these matters reached us. Now we hear from the same sources:
"Why are you so insistent with your proposals?"

This reminds me of a situation involving Hodzha Nasreddin.
As the story has it, he was riding on his donkey in Bukhara and
people were calling out at him, saying it was the first time they saw
an old donkey carrying a young one. But when Nasreddin put the
donkey on his shoulders and continued on his way, he again heard
reproaches, only now the other way round.

We think that the time has come for definitie actions. Why so?
Because we have reached a point when it is no longer enough to say:
Yes, we stand for a better world; yes, we will take the road to
normalization of the international situation. If such words are not
matched with actual deeds, we call it political demagoguery and
deception of the peoples.

In addition to those measures that the Soviet Union took unilaterally earlier, we put forward new radical proposals to impart a
constructive character to the Geneva talks. We know perhaps better
than anyone — at least not worse than the Americans — what is in

store for the world if the arms race is not stopped now. Such awareness adds to our responsiblity.

Though the situation is very tense as it is, if another round to the arms race—a space round—is initiated, I do not know if we will be able to conduct talks. How could they be approached? This should be clear to everyone. Incidentally, the press, too, should gain an understanding of the seriousness of the situation in today's international affairs. You journalists serve not only editors and those who finance your publications. You should serve the people primarily. The general demand, as we in the Soviet Union understand and feel it, is that one has to stop, gather one's wits, think of where we are, and begin to act, to take concrete steps. It is a simple formula, a simple plan, but we think that it bears responsibility for the destiny of one's people, for the destinies of the other peoples. It contains a proposal, a constructive quest. We are ready for this.

What I know about the results of the meetings of the Soviet Foreign Minister with U.S. President Reagan and Secretary of State Shultz is encouraging, to some extent. We did not hear the typical, stereotyped reply, "No, it is propaganda."

I think that sober, realistic thoughts are germinating in public opinion in the United States of America, in the political community, and in Congress. Naturally, I can hardly speak for the United States. But we hope that both in Geneva, where another round of talks has begun and where our proposals have been put on the table, and at the forthcoming meeting with President Reagan, the United States will approach that problem with a sense of serious responsibility. In this sense, I share the view of Mr. Mitterrand that there are problems that concern the Soviet Union and the United States directly and that the process of the talks should be moved from stalemate toward normalization.

The Soviet Union has a serious intention to have the world situation changed.

In the talks in Paris, we touched also upon matters of medium-range missiles. We would like to move this question away from a point at which it is hard to come to grips with it. This issue is also being discussed in Geneva, with the American side. It is a fact that Pershing and cruise missiles are being deployed in Western Europe.

Developing our position, we have made new proposals on medium-range missiles. We think—and I told Mr. Mitterrand so—that a new situation is being created in this way. Generally speaking, we have not placed and are not going to place the French nuclear forces on the "Soviet-American roster."

We are saying that this problem should be discussed with France and also with Britain. An opportunity is being opened for an exchange of opinions with France, which may lead to talks at some point.

We are not setting before France the question of a reduction in her nuclear potential, of stopping the fulfillment of her military program. That is a matter for France. As we understand it, France will approach this question from her own position, with due account for all the processes taking place in the world. But we say, "Let us start talking. Let us start studying this problem in interconnection with the others." Perhaps there could be some flexible equivalent for the corresponding nuclear systems. In any case, this is the first step. We had an in-depth exchange of views on this score with François Mitterrand. As I understand it, the President is not against continuing an exchange of views on this problem. And we, too, stand for this dialogue.

Through our ambassador in London, we have addressed a similar proposal to Mrs. Margaret Thatcher.

We also explained the essence and significance of the unilateral step that has just been taken by us and as a result of which the number of the Soviet SS-20 missiles in the European Zone now does not exceed the number that we had as of June last year. The additionally deployed SS-20 missiles have not been withdrawn from standby alert, while the permanent installations for housing these missiles will be dismantled in the next two months. Those who would like to verify this can take photographs. It is being intimated that we allegedly intend to haul these missiles to Asia. Those are unscrupulous intimations. When the Soviet Union makes a deal with somebody, it does so seriously.

We have as many missiles in Asia as are needed to balance the corresponding potential of the United States in that region—neither more nor less. If the United States does not build up, we will not build up either. If the situation changes for the better, our reaction will be adequate.

The President and I devoted much time to questions of European security. We have the experience of joint efforts with France in that field. That experience made it possible to accumulate a substantial potential for cooperation that can be used to carry on the European process based on the Helsinki Accords and to fill it with even more meaningful content.

Addressing the Parliament yesterday, I presented our position on the entire range of these problems. I will not repeat it. The crux of the matter, I think, is that both sides—the Soviet Union and France—remain committed to the cause of expanding and carrying on the European process, and the President has reiterated it now. Like France, we stand for the implementation of the provisions of the Helsinki Final Act in all its parts, and it is my profound conviction, moreover, that improvement of the situation in Europe would be vastly important to the whole world. The military-political groupings come into immediate contact in Europe. Its peoples have learned major lessons from their own history. After the Helsinki Conference, there also exists a legal base making it possible to advance on the road of cooperation and security.

The Soviet Union and France were coauthors of the Stockholm Conference. We believe that it is time to turn it more resolutely toward drafting agreements. Incidentally, as we understand it, and in the view of France, too, there are openings to invigorate the search for mutually acceptable solutions.

During the talks with President Mitterrand, we devoted proper attention to studying a number of regional problems and existing seats of tension. We have mutual understanding in the evaluation of some of these problems. As to other problems, there are differences both in analysis and approach. But we agree that such seats have to be eliminated by political means while respecting the independence and sovereignty of each country fully. And it is within such an exchange of views that we dealt with the situation in the south of Africa, the Middle East, Central America, and other problems.

We came to Paris with the desire to give a new impulse to bilateral Soviet-French relations. As I understand it, the President's position coincides with this aspiration of ours. The results of the discussion on these issues give reason to hope for an intensification of the political dialogue and a growth in economic and trade cooperation between the Soviet Union and France.

We assess positively the fact that the pace of development of economic and trade ties has quickened in recent years—they have doubled. But what we have does not accord today with the scale of the potential of our countries. That is why we have agreed to step up the search, to impart more initiative to our relations in the sphere of trade and economic cooperation. An agreement on these matters has just been signed.

Many specific interesting projects have appeared, among them several big ones. On our part, we welcome this. We think that this, too, will facilitate improvement in the overall situation.

As I have already pointed out, we have agreed to build up political dialogue. I have invited the President, on behalf of the Presidium of the USSR Supreme Soviet, to pay a visit to our country. He will be a welcome guest in the Soviet Union. When intervals between visits become shorter, perhaps there will be fewer problems. We have also exchanged opinions on the following idea: There is a project known as Tokamak. The Soviet Union, France, the United States, Japan, and other countries have contributed to the development of that project in thermonuclear synthesis. One is tempted to wonder whether this project might be carried out by joint efforts and provide a possibility for leading our research onto the road of obtaining a practically inexhaustible source of energy. It is a tempting idea. It would be timely since it is a peaceful idea—and there are those who advance very different proposals. Our specialists have told me that there are realistic hopes for the fulfillment of this proposal of ours.

On the whole, the results of the talks, in our view, are not only positive, but I would say even impressive. They serve the interests of the Soviet and French peoples, the broad interests of European and international security.

In conclusion, I would like to avail myself of the opportunity to express gratitude to President François Mitterrand, to the government, politicians and public figures of France, to all the French women and men we have met these past days, for the hospitality, and for the sentiments of affection and respect expressed by them for our country and the entire Soviet people.

Subsequently, Mikhail Gorbachev and François Mitterrand answered questions from journalists.

Question (French television Antenne-2): Mr. General Secretary, you said that the Soviet Union could not close its eyes to the development of the French nuclear forces. Do you wish that the level of the French nuclear forces would not be built up, or that it would be built up moderately? In other words, should the modernization of the French nuclear forces become, in your view, a subject for discussions with the Soviet Union?

Mikhail Gorbachev: I think I have made quite a definite statement on this question. We suggest that the process of a direct exchange of opinion be initiated. All the concrete questions can be discussed in the course of that process.

Question (Soviet Television): Mr. President, do you think it possible to achieve an international agreement blocking arms race in outer space?

François Mitterrand: I am no clairvoyant. The arms race has been rising to qualitatively new levels for a long time and has now reached the space level. If reason has not prevailed up to now, who can say that common sense will prevail today? I do not make forecasts. I have put forward a wish, a political stand: Yes, there is a need for a compromise that will be acceptable to both sides and beneficial to all. I do not want to go into technical details as to the character of such a compromise. As for the position of France, I have already said that she does not participate in it, she is not seeking it, she wants to devote herself to the peaceful exploration of space. Naturally, as a great power with a population of 55 million, she shows an interest in everything that bears on questions of war and peace.

Question (Italian newspaper *Secolo XX*): Mr. General Secretary, as I understand, you have announced the dismantling of all Soviet SS-20 missiles in excess of 243. I would like to know if you will confirm this. As to the separate agreement on medium-range missiles in Europe, do you believe it possible that a basis for this agreement can be found in what was termed in 1982 as the "agreement during the walk in the woods"?

Mikhail Gorbachev: I confirm that 243 missiles are now standing ready in the European Zone. This is exactly the same number as there were in June 1984. The other missiles have been removed, and within the next two months the permanent launching installations will be dismantled.

Our reply measures related directly to the territory of the United States remain in force. As for the further process of talks on medium-range missiles, in order to invigorate it and impart a realistic direction to this process, we have proposed a separate accord on this type of arms. And, at the same time, we proposed a direct exchange of views with France and Britain. In our opinion, this makes it possible to start practical steps. We are prepared to go in this direction as far as our partners are prepared to go—I refer to the United States and, where it concerns French and British missiles—to France and Britain.

François Mitterrand: I would like to specify: Not on a single question will France deny an exchange of views, especially to such a country as the Soviet Union. But at present I do not see possibilities for talks, although I told the General Secretary this morning that we must determine precisely the subject of discussion. I will add: As to the question of counting our forces, the United States has not distanced itself from the position of France on this matter, and France has no reason to separate its position from the American one when it comes to counting forces in the world and in Europe, with due account, of course, for everything that I have already said about outer space and for the fact that France retains full freedom to express herself and to think. We are an independent country, which has its independent strategy and which speaks out accordingly.

Question (BBC): Mr. General Secretary, I would like to touch on the Soviet Union's relations with Mrs. Thatcher. First, why, in your opinion, should the British Prime Minister take a different position on the question of Britain's medium-range nuclear systems than France? Second, have you resigned yourself to the Thatcher government's decision to expel Soviet diplomats?

Mikhail Gorbachev: For a start, I will reply to the first question. I think that so far Britain's position on medium-range missiles was formed under one set of conditions. Today I invite the President of France—and I have already done this—and Mrs. Thatcher to take a new approach in connection with the radical proposals made by the Soviet Union. This indeed changes the situation fundamentally. And if the situation is new, there should be new approaches as well. I agree with President Mitterrand—we have already discussed this with him—that it would be strange if we had begun to discuss this issue yesterday and would have entered into talks and reached accord by today. But I remember at the same time that Mr. Mitterrand, in particular during his last visit to Moscow, in presenting his position on the French nuclear forces, said that France was committed to a search for peace and to the process of disarmament. In his view, today the Soviet Union and the United States should be the first to make their contribution, which does not at all rule out that at some point France will join this process. A new situation is emerging today, and new opportunities are opening up. It was natural, on my part, to invite the President to exchange opinions on this situation.

Now I will answer your second question. Every embassy in the country to which it has been posted has instructions from its government to study processes and to supply information on processes taking place in the country in question so that there should be nothing unpredictable either in bilateral relations or on international problems. This information is, I think, a natural process. It involves all countries. If anyone wants to spoil relations and to prevent their improvement as soon as there are signs of an international dialogue, of a thaw, there immediately come to the fore forces that have their social order. They are always ready. These are "quick-response forces" intended to spoil the international situation. But who has involved Mrs. Thatcher in these affairs, when all the representatives of the Soviet Union are charged with spying en masse, I do not know.

We proceed from the assumption that the Soviet Union is interested in relations with Great Britain to no less an extent than

Britain is interested in relations with the Soviet Union. I repeat, we are for the development of relations and a political dialogue, and of economic relations with Great Britain, which is also a partner of ours of long standing. I believe this question is already exhausted.

Question (GDR Television): Comrade Gorbachev, I believe that since the Second World War, the Soviet Union has made more than a hundred proposals directed at strengthening peace and achieving disarmament. Are they still in force?

Mikhail Gorbachev: It would really be a good thing to return to some of the good old proposals: on general and complete disarmament, which was gradually driven into a corner and is now in a Cinderella position. And that, mind you, is a fundamental issue. Had attention been given in time to this proposal of ours, I am sure we would not be living through the present situation in the world. Such proposals that were of a long-term nature, and did not appear like a reaction to some current process, to some current situation, all such proposals of ours remain in force.

Question (Correspondent of Dutch television): Mr. General Secretary, could you name the number of SS-20 missiles throughout the territory of the Soviet Union? You know that the Dutch Government is to adopt a decision on November 1 on American missiles?

Mikhail Gorbachev: Your leadership is informed of our steps, and it has the chance to consider our proposals. As for information on how many missiles and of what type – I think it would take much time for me to answer this question – especially since this concerns Europe and the entire European Zone – and it goes beyond even the limits of the Urals to the 80th meridian. I think this is enough for the Netherlands.

Question (Israeli radio): You have insisted on the need for concrete steps to solve problems of seats of regional conflicts. As concerns the Middle East, wouldn't the restoration of diplomatic relations with the State of Israel be one such concrete step by the Soviet Union? If not, why?

Mikhail Gorbachev: You feel by the reaction of the hall that I do not even have to answer this question because my answer is obvious. Still I will answer your question. The situation in the Middle East is a serious one, and the President has already said it. This gives rise to concern both from the Soviet Union and from France. We will exchange views with the French leaders in search of the best solution to this problem. The Israeli leadership is pursuing a myopic policy if it wants to ensure its national interests by way of separate deals. These can be only temporary successes. The issue must be solved permanently. The Soviet Union has always taken part and will take part in a fundamental solution to the problem, in improving the entire situation in the Middle East, and will act with a sense of great responsibility in this direction so that the situation in that region will not get out of control. There must be a search for political approaches to a settlement.

There are those who have no interest in the participation of the Soviet Union. But the presence of the Soviet Union in the Middle East is an objective factor, and we do not forsake our role. We stand for collective efforts, and I share the President's view in this respect.

As for the restoration of relations with Israel, I think that the sooner the situation in the Middle East returns to normal, the quicker we can proceed to consideration of this matter. There will be no obstacles for us then. We took part in the establishment of the State of Israel. We recognize the sovereignty of that state and its right to exist and to have security. But as for how security is understood by the ruling circles of Israel and by us, we have large differences here.

Perhaps, you will put further questions to the President? (Laughter).

François Mitterrand: It is less often that they see you here. (Laughter).

Question (CBS television): Why not allow all Jews to emigrate from the Soviet Union if they wish to do so? Could you say how many political prisoners are there in the Soviet Union?

Mikhail Gorbachev: I answered these questions in my interview with French Television. I have nothing to add.

Question (French television company TF-1): You said in your speech yesterday that the world economy and technological progress called for exchanges of people and ideas. Are you planning in the near future to open the doors of the Soviet Union wider and to give Soviet people the possibility to travel freely to the West and

Westerners a possibility to come to the Soviet Union?

Mikhail Gorbachev: We feel that the Helsinki process embraces all the problems, including humanitarian ones and exchanges of ideas, information, and tourists. We fully support all this. And I think that the more the situation improves, the broader the contacts will be. On the other hand, the broader the contacts, the quicker the situation will improve. Anyway, when it does not come to attempts to use exchanges for political, provocative purposes, to poison the atmosphere and intervene in internal affairs, the doors of our country are now already open to everyone. Here is an example: A group of Americans decided to make a journey down the Volga. They came from different cities of the United States. I learned about it when they had already returned to America and were sharing their impressions of the journey. Two ships with Americans on board made a cruise along the entire Volga. You know what they said? "Everything we had known about the Soviet Union had been conditioning. And what we saw in the Soviet Union, both people and what the Soviet Union is like in general, convinces us that they are the same people as we, with the same goals, thoughts, friendliness, and aspirations." That is why, if the well-known centers do not use human communication and introduce elements which poison relations and interfere in our internal affairs, the Soviet Union stands for the development of exchanges on the basis of equality. But the Soviet Union cannot be talked to as some quarters take the liberty of talking to dozens of states and governments, thinking absolutely nothing of them. The Soviet Union will not stand for that.

Question (French radio broadcasting company Europe-1): Mr. General Secretary, when we see you, we always get good news from the Soviet Union. I would like to ask what you have told the President about Sakharov, Scharansky, and Nudel.

Mikhail Gorbachev: When it comes to the reunification of families, mixed marriages, and other humanitarian questions, these questions are considered by competent agencies in a careful manner. I said this to the President.

Question (Radio Canada): Mr. General Secretary, does the Soviet Union have a chance to avenge itself in Lebanon or to protect its citizens, or is it as helpless as the Western countries?

Mikhail Gorbachev: I think there is no reason to speak about helplessness. The influence of the Soviet Union and of other countries, including France, is tremendous in all instances, including this matter. I will say only that we are resolute opponents of terrorist methods. They are unacceptable. And we have expressed ourselves categorically on this score and have now put everything into motion that we have at our disposal to find a solution to this question. I think that those who embark on the road of terrorist methods will not achieve their aims.

Question (GDR Radio): I also have a question for the General Secretary. Here in Paris you have spoken at length about nonmilitarization of outer space. But what about peaceful cooperation in outer space? Are there new concrete plans for joint space flights, like the one three years ago?

Mikhail Gorbachev: Yes, we will continue cooperating with France along these lines. We have good experience in this respect. We have even thought about carrying out a joint flight once again. We exchanged views on this with the President. We adhere to the idea of peaceful uses and exploration of outer space. And great success can be achieved here. I have in mind our proposals at the United Nations. It would be possible to set up an organization, locate it in Paris, and launch peaceful studies of outer space.

Question (ABC television): Mr. General Secretary, you hinted in your statement this morning that there were elements of political demagoguery in the American reaction to your proposal on arms cuts. Do you mean President Reagan? If this is so, does not it contravene your statement to *Time* magazine that rhetoric should be softened up during preparations for the Geneva meeting?

Mikhail Gorbachev: I want to reiterate everything I said in the interview to representatives of *Time* magazine. I would like to note right away that the remark I made was based on the information I had received. I think it would be irresponsible to create the impression that all this is a propaganda shoot out. As for the position of Mr. Reagan, I said precisely that for the first time—I was told this by Foreign Minister Eduard Shevardnadze—we sensed on the part of the President and those who participated in the conversation, I mean Mr. Shultz, Mr. McFarlane and others, a serious attitude to our proposals. We hope that this will prove truly so. We do not want to do damage to the security of the United States. This does not enter our plans. We do not want to outplay the United States of America and advise them not to try to do so either.

Question (French journalist): Messrs. President and General Secretary, have you found common points in your positions on the Middle East, and what are they?

Mikhail Gorbachev: The President spoke about this. We are prepared to participate in an international collective search for ways to improve the situation in the Middle East. I welcome this.

Question (London *Guardian*): Do you make reducing strategic arms dependent on agreement by the United States to discontinue the development of space arms, or do you consider these issues to be interdependent? To what extent are you inclined to reach agreement with President Reagan during the meeting in Geneva?

Mikhail Gorbachev: I think that at this press conference we should not get ahead of ourselves and deal with the meeting in Geneva. After all, that is a serious matter. Both we and, I think, the American side understand this and are preparing accordingly. As to the concrete part of your question, I will say that in our opinion we must reach agreement on the nonmilitarization of space and on a radical reduction of strategic nuclear arms on earth.

Question (BBC): Mr. General Secretary, President Mitterrand has said that he is not prepared to start talks with the Soviet Union on medium-range missiles. Why?

Mikhail Gorbachev: I do not understand why you have this impression. What I was saying was that by our steps we impart movement to this process, impart dynamism to it, begin to move it off the ground, and that possibilities are opening up for contacts both with the Americans and with France and Britain.

Question (a journalist from Lebanon): The Middle East capitals are awaiting with hope and even with alarm your meeting with President Reagan. They fear its possible consequences. What place does that region hold in your priorities? What would be your reaction if the American delegation refused to discuss with you the destiny of that region, which the United States regards as it preserve? We know your principled stand on the question of Arab

territories occupied by Israel, but what would your concrete position be in practice if Syria again took up arms?

Mikhail Gorbachev: Everything taking place in the Middle
East worries us. We have never been aloof from a search for ways to
settle the situation in the Middle East on a just basis. This means that
troops must be withdrawn from occupied territories, that the Pales-
tinian problem must be resolved on the basis of self-determination,
and that the indivisibility of Lebanon and its peaceful development
and the legitimate rights of the Israeli people, the Israeli State, must
be ensured. It is in this direction that a solution must be looked for. I
think that other approaches—by separate deals and circumventing
maneuvers—can lead only to some temporary settlement, but will
not produce a solution to the problem so that a lasting peace in the
Middle East can be created. That is why collective efforts are
needed to search for truly realistic ways out of the situation. And as
to what the Americans think to be a sphere of their "vital interests,"
as you say, it is they who think so. The Americans claim "vital
interests" now here, now there. Let the Americans think about that
formula.

Meanwhile, this is one of the factors leading to misunderstand-
ing and acute situations. If one announces that everything in the
world is a zone of one's "vital interests," what will be left for the
other peoples? For two hundred nations? The status of vassals, or
what? This does not at all accord with the concept of equal development of the peoples and with the possibility for every people to
exercise their sovereign rights and to make their own choice. This
process often proceeds painfully.

We make no secret of our position. When people in one country
or another choose a road of progressive change and seek to formu-
late an independent policy, to mold their own outlook in the spiritual
field and to establish their own economic institutions, we welcome
this. We are on the side of those peoples. But as soon as we say so, it
is stated: "The hand of Moscow, the hand of Moscow!"

International relations are being practiced in a changeable and
multifaceted world in the context of political, cultural, and economic development at different levels of progress. And we should
take every step with great responsibility. It is inadmissible to pro-

ceed from imperialistic considerations. I apply this also to the
Soviet Union. We have never allowed and will not allow this to
happen.

October 4, 1985